What Readers Say:

"...you've put the cookies on the lower shelf and given us much needed clarity about the significant role family philanthropy plays in the development of a child's values...this is also the finest age-appropriate guide to giving I've read."

Dan Rice, National Director of Gift Planning,
World Vision

"...this book should be found in family libraries everywhere."

Christina Wilson, Executive Director,
Rancho Santa Fe Foundation

"This book eloquently illustrates how to use family philanthropy in teaching values and accountability... so important to the post-transition management of family wealth and unity."

Bill Bone, President of a Canadian Foundation &
Family Office

"...your book hits it square on...A very valuable work...Important for one's Heirs."

Glen A. Holden, U.S. Ambassador, Glen & Gloria
Holden Family Foundation

"...Responsible philanthropy is a learned skill. Roy and Vic's newest book will be helpful as families initiate this educational journey."

Art & Sarah Ludwick, Ludwick Family Foundation

"...children properly involved in philanthropy can learn a great deal about the importance of values, the need for mission clarity, and the requirement for follow-up accountability."

Lynn Booth, Director,
Clement and Lynn Hirsch Foundation

"...our family foundation taught my brother, sister and me the benefits of a common mission, and the cohesion it brought to our post-transition generation."

Joe Harper, Director of the
Cecil B. DeMille Foundation

"...your research proves what we've practiced for years...and the book spells out "how to" for all age groups."

Don Oliphant, Past Chair, Rancho Santa Fe
Foundation and Director Knott's Berry Farms Foods

"...the heart of not only philanthropy, but life itself... to produce healthy heirs in generation after generation."

Fred Smith, President, The Gathering

"The book is especially helpful to me at this time as I am having difficulty moving the family to the next stage (building for when I am gone and rearranging direction)... it is a good book"

John E. McCutcheon, President,
McCutcheon Family Foundation

"...your coaching of our family with respect to involving the children really paid off... they (our 3 children, their cousins and, respective spouses) are members, accountable to each other, with clear responsibilities... and they are all learning and growing."

Dick Boyd, Boyd Family Foundation

"...right on target! This book proves that philanthropy is an incredible teaching tool for your family once you know how to apply its power."

Bill Lane, Founder: "Sunset Magazine"

"...a timely primer...that helps to correct the problem ...of successful family businesses going under because the next generation wasn't prepared."

General P. X. Kelley, 28th Commandant-USMC
Chairman, Air Warrior Courage Foundation

"...This book is a great tool for preparing the 3rd generation and as a refresher for those of us who started with 'Preparing Heirs'."

Jim & Becky Morgan, Morgan Family Foundation

"This book should be the handbook for all philanthropic advisors throughout the country."

Don Hartmann, Director NAPP/NAFWC
(to become "International Association of Advisors in Philanthropy" April 2005)

This book is dedicated to

Kristin Nowell

Who joined the ranks

of strong women

when she established

her own foundation to save

the wild cats of the world

Cat Action Treasury - 1996

Philanthropy, Heirs & Values

How Successful Families
Are Using Philanthropy
To Prepare Their Heirs For
Post-Transition Responsibilities

Roy Williams & Vic Preisser

Robert D Reed Publishers
PO Box 1992, Bandon, OR 97411
Phone: 541-347-9882 Fax 9883
E-Mail 4bobreed@msn.com
Web Site www.rdrpublishers.com

Philanthropy, Heirs, & Values

Library of Congress Control Number: 2004099568

ISBN 1-931741-51-4   5½ x 8½; hard cover; $29.95

The Williams Group
website: thewilliamsgroup.org
3620 W. Hammer Lane, Stockton, CA 95219
Phone: 209-477-0600

Disclaimer:

CONTENTS:

Acknowledgements

Many thanks to those who took the time, and made the effort to give us the feedback on our research and our conclusions. Some of them are listed as endorsers in the front of the book.

And, we are grateful to the families who let us into their homes, their private thoughts, and their concerns for their children. We appreciate your confidence in us, and we respect your wish for privacy.

Ultimately, this book can only be as beneficial as the foundation managers, and the advisory and estate planning professionals who decide to tell their client families of its existence. We acknowledge the great job you are doing, and we look forward to assisting you as you introduce your clients and supporters to Post-Transition planning.

Thank you all for giving successful families one more good reason to support philanthropy.

Roy and Vic

Chapter 1

Introduction

We specialize in *post-transition* planning, preparing heirs for receipt of wealth and responsibility. (Estate Planners generally handle *pre-transition* planning.) Preparing heirs has been our focus for the past 40+ years, not philanthropy. However, in that process we have learned much from thousands of financially successful families around the world. Data on these families have been accumulated, sorted, and analyzed by The Leadership Family Institute[1]. During the last 20 years of research it became increasingly obvious that some families are "ahead of the curve" in preparing their heirs for wealth and responsibility. *Some of that preparation resulted from deliberately using family philanthropy as a teaching device to prepare their heirs.* We went back to the families themselves to learn exactly how they used philanthropy.

We are not theorists. We are not academics. We are pragmatists concerned with what successful (post-transition) families did *to prepare for* their transition. This book spells out the surprising opportunities for children to learn, practice, and solidify family values through appropriate involvement in philanthropy. Of course, children/heirs will develop values regardless of what the parents do, or fail to do. However, if

---

[1] The Leadership Family Institute is a non-profit tax-exempt organization that studies the problems facing the children of successful families, and provides education and training for the families and heirs (and spouses) to improve their odds of success and family harmony in future generations.

the correct parental values are conveyed, the odds of that next generation becoming successful are greatly increased.

Improving the upcoming generation's chances for success through planned involvement in the family's philanthropy is the focus of this book. This is not intended to diminish the practice or goals of philanthropy. It is, rather, meant to introduce *an additional usage* for philanthropy... a usage internal to the family and for the benefit of the family's upcoming generation. And with 70,000 private foundations in the United States and Canada (controlling $500+ billion in assets), this is not an insignificant opportunity.

Certainly it will have the added benefit of introducing many heirs to the practice of philanthropy, expanding the rationale for philanthropy well beyond obvious tax reasons. With philanthropy identified as *an effective tool in the development of heirs*, philanthropy will become an even more important element in the family's life and plans. Faced with only 30% odds[2] of a successful post-transition experience, families are seeking every tool that will improve on those frightening odds. Philanthropy is one of those tools that, until now, were *effectively* applied by very few families.

The Williams Group studied 3,000+ transitioning families and almost 100 family foundations in an effort to understand how families used their philanthropic activities to develop their heirs

---

[2] See Appendix B

while serving their charitable passion. A clear pattern emerged.

Children form their own values based upon what they see being modeled by their parents. While a family foundation/philanthropy is only one element in their overall development, it turns out to be one of the more important elements for children in affluent families. Why? Because involvement of the child in family philanthropy provides the heir with an entire series of observable and understandable "interfaces" between the child's family and the family's relationship to the outside world... the interface between the child's family environment, and the environment of others. An interface between the child's assumptions of the "always correct adult" and early awareness of the (sometimes) "neglectful, forgetful, and inattentive adult." And, a transition from the child's view of "we are all kind of equal" to the adult view of "we are all valuable individuals."

Teaching Moments in Philanthropy

Perhaps equally startling was the awareness that some parents had concerning "teachable moments" for their heirs. Some parents saw those teachable moments in many places, including activities with and around the family's philanthropy. Most parents, busy with the dozens of needs to simply navigate their family through the day, had other concerns commanding their attention. *Regardless of parental outlook, the child's observational skills and learning did not wait for deliberate parental guidance.* The children learned values, no matter what the parent did, or did not do. The differences were found in the values that were learned, the quality of learning, and the *sources* for the values learned. The use of family philanthropy provided a special learning opportunity that had a surprising and enduring impact on the development of those learned values.

40 Years of Post-Transition Planning

We at The Williams Group have spent the past 40 years advising families on how to prepare for the impact of wealth upon their heirs. Our findings are based upon our unique research, and direct experience with thousands of affluent families. When one examines what affluent parents worry about, it isn't only their money, or taxes. They worry about the impact of wealth upon their children. They know affluence can be a power for good, or a power for destruction in the life of an heir. Regardless, affluence has impact beyond the heir, and the heir's family. Wealth is a magnifier of what is right, and also what is wrong. So much depends upon how families have prepared their children for responsibility. So, it is with great care that we have researched and written books about the intergenerational transfer of wealth (*"For Love & Money"* © 1997) and evaluating a family's readiness to transition wealth and values (*"Preparing Heirs"* ©2003)[3]. This book is an extension of our research, our experience, and our focus on preparing those who have a special burden of inherited responsibility.

---

[3] The books and measurement tools for your family may be seen on the website: *thewilliamsgroup.org* and Appendix F

Giving Did Not Begin Because of Tax Reasons

Before the end of the 19th century, the Rockefeller family hired a professional "Philanthropical Advisor." Income taxes in the USA began later, during the early 20th century. Thus, philanthropy did not begin for tax reasons. Originally, philanthropy was seen as "giving back" to the community. As income tax rates increased, and "taxable income" became more precisely defined (because government didn't want to extinguish private philanthropy) tax planning began to be more influenced by the concept of *"voluntary giving"* (to one's philanthropic cause of choice) versus *"involuntary giving"* (to the IRS). During that shift, the financial advisors for many family foundations occasionally lost sight of the original reasons for giving. Recently, with ups and downs in the marketplace, families are re-examining their *desire* to give, the *amount* they give, and in some cases, the *rationale* for giving at all. It is in that spirit of re-examination that The Williams Group researched family foundations in order to see if they could discover benefits from a family foundation or family philanthropy beyond the "giving back to the community" aspect.

The Role of Family Philanthropy in Setting Values in Heirs

Where heirs were encouraged, and intelligently guided to participate in family philanthropy, it had a profound impact in three major areas of their development and preparation for later life. The three major areas were discovered to be **Values, Mission** and **Accountability**.

By *"Values"* we mean those beliefs that become foundational to the heir's attitude towards money as a determinant of self. In short, properly handled, family philanthropy plays a major role in *separating* the child's sense of self-esteem from the amount of money involved in the child's life. Family philanthropy, properly taught (and modeled), established that money did not determine "who" a child was. With properly developed values, children embraced the viewpoint of money as a tool, not a self-definer, thus having a positive impact on their self-esteem.

By *"Mission"* we mean that awareness developed by the heir concerning what the family wanted to *accomplish* with their family wealth. Seen by involved heirs as a tool, money became a lever towards achieving a unified mission, building family coherence, family strength, and public propagation of the family's values. As these took place, the potential of money as a "divider" receded into the background.

Finally *"Accountability"* was the third major factor strengthened by the involvement of heirs in family philanthropy. It seems that philanthropy, at least for the early formative years of heirs, is seen by heirs in very real terms. When money is given on behalf of philanthropy, it is expected to go to *precisely* the usage that the young heir/donor intends. Young donors are very much taken aback, by any reasons given, if *all* of the funds did not go for the *specifically* designated purpose. Accordingly, there is an innate sense of accountability in young heirs, and affirming that sense turns out to be important and readily attainable. Family philanthropy turns out to be a surprisingly effective mechanism for that affirmation... and accountability turns out to be one of the keys for success in managing wealth/self as an adult.

Structure of the Book

This book focuses upon reinforcing each of these three major areas, dependent upon the *age of the heir*. Put in simple terms, you do different things (as a parent) to reinforce accountability for a 10-year-old heir, than you do for the 25-year-old heir. The five major age periods addressed throughout this book are consistent with the major developmental periods for young people and adults. And, we categorize them as follows:

Ages 5-10   *Awakening Years*, discovering one's personal influence

Age 11-15   *Exploring Years*, discovering self in the midst of change

Age 16-20   *Developing Years*, understanding accountability

Age 21-30   *Applying Years*, maximizing the value of contributions

Beyond 30   *Mentoring Years*, unifying the family through Philanthropy

How to Use this Book

First, families need to comprehend the *stunningly high failure rate* that follows the transition of wealth to heirs. This is a worldwide

phenomenon that hovers around the 70% level[4].
Despite the best intentions of families and the
skill of estate planners, trust officers, and
financial advisors, the transferred wealth is
dissipated in 70% of the cases. While getting
wealth to and through the (tax) barriers is the
focus of pre-transition planning, little is done in
the field of post-transition planning. Wealth
often becomes a source of friction and dispute
within the family, for causes that literally have
nothing to do with tax planning. The causes
behind these phenomena, and how to assess your
own family's situation, are reviewed in the
Chapter 3. It is not our theory of "how to fix it"
that is presented. What you will read is how
3,250 affluent study-group families (who made
the transition) behaved following their transition.
Seventy percent lost control of their assets and
family unity, and only 30% succeeded. The
differences between the two groups of families
are quite instructive and a convenient checklist is
presented for your family's use.

Second, Chapter 2 deals with the most common
basis for family philanthropy. Focus is given to
the country which gives a larger proportion of its
income to charity than any other country in the
world... the USA. With 7,000 families, each
transitioning over $20 million every year, the
USA attracts the most detailed forecasts of
philanthropy of any country in the world.

Third, The actual research by The Williams
Group into the causes of post-transition failure
and their relationship to family foundations are

---

4 See Appendix B

reviewed in Chapter 4. The impact of philanthropy upon their heirs is reviewed in some detail. However, the procedures that parents/families used to apply those "learning opportunities" to heirs are organized in Chapters 5 through 9 of this book. Those chapters are written in the present tense for understandability as the reader seeks guidance. Other sections of the book are written in the past tense as they refer to research findings.

Chapter 4 is the "...if you have to skip everything else, go directly to..." this chapter. It is built around the tools of assessment (is your family most like those who succeeded or like those who failed?), and how does philanthropy help prepare your heirs? Preparation for what? Preparation for wealth and responsibility, and preparing them for three major areas that will have a major impact throughout their adult life:

- What are our family **VALUES**?

- How do you define a **MISSION** for the family wealth, and how do we use philanthropy in support of that mission?

- How are the charitable recipients held **ACCOUNTABLE** for its effective usage, its coherence with our family mission, and its consistency with our family values?

It is our hope that this book will serve as a ready reference for the family leadership at various times during discussions/assignments on family philanthropy.

Chapter 10 of this book is one of self-measurement. How does one measure the readiness of heirs to assume responsibility for the intelligent and enlightened management of wealth? We can assure you that the criterion is not an MBA from Stanford or Harvard. The criteria relates more often to matters of the heart, and solid judgment than to skills of the mind. Ultimately it is accelerated by mentorship. All of us had parents as mentors. The effectiveness of mentoring from parents or any other source is ultimately a matter of the quality, relevance, availability, and consistency of that mentoring that determines its impact. The research is underway at this moment for the fall 2005 release of our next book, *"Mentoring Heirs."*©2005

Chapter 2

Philanthropy in the USA

A Spirit of Generosity

In the USA there are approximately 77,000 philanthropic organizations, both private and public. Most private philanthropies were stimulated by good tax reasons. The simple tax advisor's question: "...do you want to give to *your* charity of choice, or to the *government's agency* of choice?" proved to be a powerful stimulus to (tax-exempt) foundation formation. The tax code itself encouraged the formation of tax-exempt foundations and non-profit organizations, further stimulating philanthropic considerations during the planning for transfer of family assets. Historical records show that, for all the criticism the USA receives, it is still one of the most generous nations in the world. Seen as a portion of the Gross Domestic Product, the data reveals the following:

COUNTRY	PROPORTION OF THE GROSS DOMESTIC PRODUCT (ALL GOODS AND SERVICES IN 1995) FOR PHILANTHROPIC CONTRIBUTIONS[5]
United States	100 = 1% of GDP
Britain	60
Argentina	40
France	30
Brazil	18
Japan	15
Germany	14
Mexico	5

Wealth to be Transferred During the Next 50 Years

The most recent calculations of "personally held wealth" rely heavily upon estimates made by the Federal Reserve. The Federal Reserve defines "Wealth" as homes, personal assets, business holdings, real property, stocks, and bonds, cash on deposit, etc. The Federal Reserve's estimate in 1998[6] cited a figure of $37 trillion. Since 1998, changes in valuation, economic growth, and monetary inflation have combined to increase

[5] John Hopkins Comparative Non-Profit Sector Report for 1995. 100 = 1% of The Named Country's GDP
[6] Issue #5, Sept/Oct 1999 of *The Economy In Action*, Federal Reserve Bank of Dallas

that figure by at least 3% every year. In the year 2004, the amount of "personally held wealth" is probably closer to $45 trillion. This 3% figure does not take into account the actual growth (and declines) in the Stock Market during that same interval.

Wealth Awaiting Transfer

The amount of personally held wealth expected to be forfeited to taxes, and how much is available to the beneficiaries (and philanthropies) *after* taxes, have been the subject of a number of studies. In the Fall of 2004, Forbes Magazine reported 340 billionaires with USA, Canadian or Mexican citizenship[7]. Perhaps the most comprehensive study of wealth transfer forecasting was recently assembled by the Social Welfare Research Institute of Boston College[8]. Their study was done as part of estimating how much philanthropies might expect to receive in future contributions.

That study estimated the transfer of wealth during the 50-year period between 1998-2052. The amount of wealth to be transferred varied with the Institute's assumptions concerning economic growth rates, taxation levels, etc. The study made "High," "Middle," and "Lower" estimates of the amount of money that would be passed on to beneficiaries each year for the next 50 years.

---

[7] Forbes Magazine, October 2004, data based on statistics from February 4, 2002. Based on US $.
[8] "The New Physics of Philanthropy," Paul G. Shervish, et al, April 11, 2001

Wealth Transfer 1998-2052

(US $, USA only)

High Estimate	$90 Trillion
Middle Estimate	**$52 Trillion**
Lower Estimate	$31 Trillion

Obviously, the range of estimated outcomes varies widely. This book uses "Middle Estimates" throughout. Counting ONLY estates with a *net value of $1 million or more*, the summary numbers using the middle estimate are as follows:

Wealth Transfer 1998-2052

Mid-Range Estimate (US $, USA only)

AVERAGE

Number of Estates that transition	1.8 Million/yr
$ Value of Estates (before Fees & Taxes)	$1.5 Trillion/yr
$ Value Transferred to Heirs & Philanthropy	$1.0 Trillion/yr
$ Value Transferred to Philanthropy	**$250 Billion/yr**

Of the $52 trillion transferred after fees and taxes, *approximately 25%, or about $12 trillion is anticipated to be distributed to philanthropic causes during this 50 year period, either during the donor's* *lifetime or as part of the bequest at time of wealth transfer.*[9]

This transfer represents an enormous and underutilized opportunity for influencing the developmental readiness of heirs. In fact, **the USA can expect to experience the transition of 7,000 estates each year, each having a value in excess of $20 million.** If only 30% "succeed," then this means almost 5,000 estates each year will lose both assets and family unity.

The responsibility of changing this truly disappointing post-transition percentage rate falls upon designated heirs, trustees, or professional managers (prepared or not and whether they share the family's values or not). This responsibility is then redistributed (consciously or subconsciously) across the families (via influencers such as spouses, partners, children, siblings, etc.) of the heirs, as well as their professional advisors.

Who Prepares Heirs for Wealth and Responsibility?

Family leaders who make plans to transition wealth are ultimately concerned about its impact on the lives and well being of *their* heirs/beneficiaries. Our studies indicated that patriarchs and matriarchs shared a similar set of questions and concerns, regardless of whether they were bequeathing liquid assets, businesses, real property, or other combinations. "What difference will the wealth make in the lives of our

---

[9] This is based on assumptions that the rate/proportion of philanthropic giving remains stable.

children and grandchildren?" "Will the family's values be transmitted along with the wealth, and reflected in how the wealth is used?" "How will wealth impact the communities in which the children live?"

Clearly, answering these questions about successful families is not a priority for educational, religious, or most research institutions. In fact, there are very few resources that focus on the preparation of heirs, and how to equip them to be good stewards and thoughtful administrators[10]. Given the potential for wealth to be used for good or ill (or simply to be "wasted" with no detectable impact), the preparation of heirs to manage wealth becomes one of the more important responsibilities successful parents face. The question becomes: "How well prepared are those heirs and *their* families?" Because, in the final measure, the quality of preparation (of the heirs) forms the answer to the central concern in the mind of every parent: "Will this wealth help or harm my family?"

Preparing heirs requires a broad spectrum of study and experience. It is not accomplished simply by sending heirs off to college, or even to a specialized business school to learn finance and economics... thereafter returning to work in the management of the family assets. Learning how to remain sensitive to (and apply) the family's

---

[10] The tax-exempt /non-profit Leadership Family Institute founded by The Williams Group performs long-term mentoring and training of leaders/heirs who anticipate assuming responsibility for the oversight of family holdings.

values, and to do it within the highly competit_ve marketplace challenging the family assets is fundamental.

The *mission* for the family's wealth, if it is to remain steady into the next generation, should be a broadly developed *consensus* mission with the participation (and ultimate agreement or acceptance) by *all family members and spouses.* Attainment of this *mission,* accompanied by routine reporting on progress (i.e., *accountability*) towards the family mission, has demonstrably built trust and communication within the family and community. That sense of family harmony around a shared mission models behaviors for younger heirs. In turn that provides heirs with a sense of family mission that carries over into the subsequent generation.

> The Binghams of Louisville could not resolve a dispute between a sister, Sallie Bingham, and her brother, Barry Bingham Jr.
>
> Sallie wanted to sell shares in the company after being "snubbed" by Barry. He was named by their father to run the family's newspapers, television and radio stations.
>
> Without a shared mission, and unable to resolve the dispute, eventually, and reluctantly, Barry Sr. sold their $430 million media dynasty in 1986 to settle the issue of fairness by using cash.
> USA Today 1/5/2003

Chapter 3

The Failure Rate in Estate Transitions

Preparing for Transition

For generation after generation, worldwide, about 70% of estates fail following their transition into the hands of heirs. By fail, we mean that the heirs have involuntarily lost control of the transferred assets. This occurs through poor investments, dissipation through arguments and legal expenses, inattention and lack of preparation/qualification for asset management, and a number of other causes. In fact, around the world there are various "traditional" phrases that refer to this inter-generational failure to retain or grow assets, such as:

- *"Fu Bu Guo San Dai[11]"*
- *"Dalle stalle, alle stelle, alle stalle"*
- *"Quien no lo tiene, lo hace,*
  y quien lo tiene, lo deshace"
- *"Clogs to clogs in Three Generations"*
- *"Rice Bowl to Rice Bowl in ..."*
- *"Rags to riches to rags"*
- *"Shirtsleeves to Shirtsleeves..."*

The 70% estate attrition experience has been confirmed several times by major studies[12] but it was not until recently that research confirmed the underlying causes.

---

[11] China: "Wealth never survives 3 generations"; Italy: "From the stalls to the stars to the stalls"; Spain: "Those who don't have it, make it, and those have it lose it"
[12] The widely varied sources are shown in Appendix B of this book, and are supported by the direct experience of the 3,250 families interviewed by The Williams Group.

Facts Underlying the 70% Failure Rate
Following Transition

The Williams Group conducted a study of 3,250 families who transitioned their wealth. Those interviews focused upon the differences between "successful" heirs and "unsuccessful" heirs in their post-transition environment. We discovered, to our surprise, that there was *no relationship between post-transition failure and tax laws, geography, culture, economic cycles, wars, or any other economic parameters.*

It was also confirmed that professional advisors from the legal, accounting, and financial management professions were *rarely the cause of any post-transition losses or failure to transfer.* In fact, setting aside the issues of economic efficiency, *the estate planning professions consistently performed their planning and legal tasks well.*

In short, the money transitioned well, but the families did not.

Much *less* time was spent on planning the transition of the *family*, than on the transition of the family *assets*. In fact, that imbalance is exactly why an annual survey by the US Trust company revealed[13] that parents worry *most* about their post-transition environment for the heirs... not the assets themselves! The "Top 6 Parental Concerns" of the surveyed families (before the transition) were as follows:

---

[13] US Trust Survey XIX, December 2000

Top Parental Concerns (About Heirs)[14]

60%   *"Too Much Emphasis on Material Things"*

55%   *"Naïve About the Value of Money"*

52%   *"Spend Beyond Their Means"*

50%   *"Initiative Ruined by Affluence"*

49%   *"Won't Do as Well Financially…"*

42%   *"Hard Time Taking Financial Responsibility"*

As we spoke with the families it became apparent that their worries and concerns about their children were valid. Not because their children/heirs were "bad kids," but because there was *no post-transition planning or preparation going on!* Extraordinarily, the assets were receiving all the attention from the professionals. Tax advisors, investment specialists, trust officers, and legal experts were all focused upon the assets. That made sense because assets were countable, transferable, and manageable. They "did what they were told." The forces opposing management (taxing authorities, competitors, creditors, weak investment markets, etc.) were all well defined and could be planned for.

Heirs were less responsive to (parental) management. They couldn't be "told" what to do to protect themselves, and then be managed into that configuration. Accordingly, when asked about the things that worry them most, parents focused on their children (heirs) and their feeling of the heir's (insufficient) preparedness for wealth and responsibility.

---

[14] Totals exceed 100% because parents often voiced more than one concern to the US Trust survey.

Separating Families into Two Groups

The major insight came when The Williams Group separated the **post-transition** families into two groups – *successful* (at retaining and building their assets and maintaining family unity) and *unsuccessful* (by losing or dissipating their assets with an accompanying loss of family unity). The 3,250 research families separated into two groups in proportions similar to those observed and reported worldwide; one group of 1,000 (successful) post-transition families and the second group of 2,250 (unsuccessful) post-transition families… approximately the 30% - 70% split traditionally experienced. Then, by carefully identifying the differences between the two researched groups, a pattern clearly emerged which highlighted unexpected factors strongly influencing the success of *post-transition estates*. Summarized in matrix form, the following major distinctions stood out:

MAJOR DIFFERENCES IN
POST TRANSITION OUTCOMES
SUCCESSFUL   *vs.*   *UNSUCCESSFUL*

Entire family (including heirs & spouses) had reached consensus on a long-term **Mission for the family wealth,** as well as the Strategy and Roles necessary to attain the Mission.	Parents only (working with professional advisors) designed the estate transition, **focusing upon the traditional elements of taxation, preservation and governance (control).**
Heirs (and spouses) participated in **defining their post-transition roles and responsibilities,** and took responsibility for preparing to assume their roles.	Heirs **discovered their responsibilities at the time of the estate transfer,** with widely varying role experiences prior to that time. Spouses not involved.

When these major distinctions were summarized, it became evident that what distinguished successful post-transition families was their focus on their children, preparing and involving them for the post-transition, a sense of family unity, confidence that they all knew what they faced (with the family estate), and that there were no hidden agendas about "their individual interests." *The family had unified around a common mission, common values, and shared a sense of 'authentic trust'[15] in one another.* Spouses were

---

15 Authentic trust, common mission, and common values are the 3 requirements for family or team unity over the long term. Our research clearly shows that if *any one* of these 3

fully included partners in the family meetings, which were held regularly. Family holidays were separate from family business meetings. "Surprises" were few and far between for successful post-transition families due to the high levels of trust and information exchange within the family *prior* to the transition. Successful post-transition families had developed the capacity and accumulated training/experience to work through the normal difficulties that crop up following every transition[16].

"10 Critical *(pre-transition)* Elements" that Separate Successful vs. Unsuccessful Families

As an outcome of the research, and as detailed on page 57 of the book "*Preparing Heirs*©2003," there were 10 questions that strikingly differentiated successful (post-transition) transition families from those families who were not successful in the post-transition phase.

Those families who answered, "Yes" to 7 *or more* of the following questions *before the transition* were most likely to be a post-transition *success* story[17]. Those who answered, "Yes" to 3 *or fewer questions* were highly likely to have been members of the *unsuccessful* post transition group. Following the study, we observed a number of families with "Yes" answers to only 4,

---

[16] These unpredictable "normal difficulties" are often referred to as "bumps in the road," and offer significant opportunities for the family to learn, cooperate, and bond.
[17] 95+% confidence level in the prediction from the 10 questions

5 or 6 of the questions who, alerted to the risk, gathered their family together to improve their odds of post-transition success. With surprisingly little effort, they "reversed" their odds of failure by involving their entire family in a professionally coached transition preparation process.

The 10 elements that emerged to most strongly identify and separate the 30%(successful)-70% (unsuccessful) division were as follows:

The researcher's attention was attracted by the differentiating questions 3, 7, and 8 with their implications for the involvement of the children in the family philanthropy. Questions that dealt with "..All family members have the option of participating..." and "...includes creating incentives and opportunities for heirs.." and "younger children are encouraged to participate in the family's philanthrop(ies)." gave the implication that the families felt that outside charitable involvement was important, and that learning could begin at an early age.

It was an examination of these inferences that led to the further research into the specific impact (on heirs) of family philanthropy. It revealed that family philanthropy was an excellent opportunity to set **values** (early on), reinforce a sense of **mission**, and awaken **accountability** expectations as families strove to develop competent heirs.

Questioning the Readiness of Heirs, and The Self-Preparation Efforts of Heirs

In the book *"Preparing Heirs"*©2003 there are two additional sets of clearly differentiating questions

TEN CRITICAL PRE-TRANSITION
ELEMENTS (1st Checklist of 3)

1. Our family has a mission statement that spells out the overall purpose of our wealth.

2. The entire family participates in most important decisions, such as defining a mission for our wealth.

3. All family heirs have the option of participating in the management of the family's assets.

4. Heirs understand their future roles, have "bought into" those roles, and look forward to performing in those roles.

5. Heirs have actually reviewed the family's estate plans and documents.

6. Our current wills, trusts, and other documents make most asset distributions based upon heir readiness, not heir age.

7. Our family mission includes creating incentives and opportunities for our heirs.

8. Our younger children are encouraged to participate in our family's philanthropic grant-making decisions.

9. Our family considers family unity to be just as important as family financial strength.

10. We communicate well throughout our family and regularly meet as a family to discuss issues and changes.

for estates evaluating their likelihood of success as they approached transition. The two additional question sets focused on two related aspects:

A 10 Question **"Heir Readiness Checklist"** *for parents and owners* (2nd Checklist) of enterprises about to transition their estates and responsibility. This checklist specifically examines the heir (as opposed to the entire estate) as to whether or not the *heir* is prepared for pot-transition responsibilities. (p. 112 of *"Preparing Heirs"* ©2003)

A 10 Question **"Heir Readiness Self-Checklist"** *for heir*s (3rd Checklist) so the heir can fairly evaluate *his/her own personal efforts* as transition responsibilities approach. (p. 138 of *"Preparing Heirs"* ©2003)

The three major "differentiating questionnaires" mentioned above are not theoretical. They are the clearest differentiators between those families who are likely to have a post-transition successful outcome (retention and growth of assets, family unity, etc.) and those families who are likely to experience an unsuccessful post-transition outcome. In turn, as good differentiators, *they are also excellent predictors of whether or not an entire family will be successfully unified during post-transition.*

The obvious shortcoming of the three 10 question sets is that they are based upon the *assessment* of one person. Dad or Mom (each) have their own (individual) opinion for each question. An individual opinion of the level of readiness of *the heir...* or of the *family's* level of understanding of the "mission for the family wealth." *Those individual assessments may substantially differ from the opinions of others in the same family, and absent a more comprehensive survey may give off with a false alarm or a false note of comfort.*

Dad may think the mission is perfectly clear, because he has repeated it so many times over the years. But Dad's spoken words, and their understood meaning, when placed (by the heir) in the context of how their heir's life and family are evolving, may be understood in a completely different context than dad intended. This often led to dramatically different conclusions for the heir(s), their spouses, as to whether or not the family was prepared for the post-transition future. It is this difference in understanding between *parentally described "futures"* and the *heir's "unconfirmed expectations" and "sense of entitlements"* that underlies the surprisingly low post-transition 30% success rate.

To remove dependence upon any one person's assessment, it became clear that the entire family needed to be polled... including spouses and of-age children (16 and older). How does the *entire family* assess the family's readiness for transition? Did they all *share the same assessment* as the parents? If the parent thought the heir was "ready," did the heir share that assessment? And, "ready" for what assignment or future role? In response to this need for a broader family-wide assessment, *The Williams Group* developed a **50 Question Family-Wide survey**. To ensure accurate responses from family members, the family survey respondents had to be assured of anonymity (especially spouses, who did not want to be seen as contentious, overly-curious, or disruptive). This anonymously-answered survey is now available for completion by *all adult family members and spouses/partners*, and *children over 15 years of age*, with their unsigned (anonymous) answers returned directly to the Williams Group for scoring. The **Family Wide Survey**[18] then generates a written report for the entire family which addresses the following:

1. Whether or not some family members see their readiness (for post-transition) quite differently than the other family members

2. Whether the family is, overall, likely to succeed, or to fail, in the post-transition environment

3. The specific areas of skill and behavior, internal to the family, that should be focused on to dramatically increase the family's odds of post-transition success

This family-wide survey has demonstrated remarkable precision in its ability to *reveal differences within the family*, and precisely where those differences lie... without compromising confidentiality within the family member answers[19].

Summarizing, there are a number of tools that now allow families to *compare their state of*

---

[18] This Family-Wide Survey is available through the process described in Appendix F of this book.

[19] The Family-Wide Survey is discussed in more detail in *"Preparing Heirs"*©2003 on pages 82 through 89.

transition readiness to families who have transitioned before. Then, comparing their answers to families who have gone before, the family can gain a remarkably accurate insight into the post-transitional environment likely to be faced by the inheriting generation. It is then the family's pre-transition option as to precisely what remedial or reinforcing actions to take. The use of family philanthropy to reinforce important **values** in heirs, and the strengthening of a sense of **mission,** turns out to be two of the more important factors identified by the Survey.

Chapter 4

Failure Causes and Philanthropy

Philanthropy is "big business." What does that mean for the long term success of your family and your children (heirs and spouses and grandchildren)? According to first 91 family foundations we separately interviewed,[20] the family foundation/philanthropy can make a big difference in the readiness and self esteem of the heir(s). In fact, it may be one of the most overlooked tools available to families in preparing their heirs for wealth and responsibility. We have learned that the development of competence in a child, leads to confidence in that child, and confidence naturally leads to a gain in self-esteem within that child. Those findings are consistent.

Philanthropy can be one of those activities (among many others such as academic achievement, sports, the arts, etc.) that should be made appropriate for various age and maturity levels. For most families, philanthropy is a learning process. The fact that the heir can share in that learning, and see that parents are learning at the same time they are, is comforting to heirs. That shared learning, where all parties are "beginners," allows the removal of pretensions and the intimacy that stems from shared personal growth.

---

[20] See Appendix A for a fuller discussion of the research.

Research into successful post-transition families has continually reinforced our belief in the accuracy of the following assertion:

> *"A team (family) that does not share common values, common mission and authentic trust will not remain together over the long term."*

Successful post-transition is built around bringing the above assertion to life for an individual family. Whether or not they articulated it in that precise phraseology, *successful* post-transition families emphasized the following *prior* to their estate transition:

1. **Total family involvement** (both spouses and bloodline)

2. A **process that integrates** what the family members learn together.

3. The **teaching and practical application (in family situations) of skills** in the areas of:

   a. communication
   b. openness
   c. trust
   d. accountability
   e. team (family) consensus building
   f. articulating shared values
   g. sharing a common mission

The involvement of the entire family proved to be one of the key differences defining successful post-transition families. While more difficult and time consuming, it avoided the trap of Mom or Dad trying to dictate "the future" to their children. Our research indicated quite clearly that when Mom or Dad *privately decided* what is to be done with the transitioned wealth, it simply did not work. The advent of their deaths often revealed open disagreement among the siblings. Each sibling held his/her own opinions about what should be done with the family wealth, and felt they hadn't been consulted. This revealed a divergence in generational unity, with each heir pulling hard in their own direction... and with little understanding or allegiance to the parent's pre-transition perspective. In these situations, the only unifying factor that the siblings often shared was agreement on funding the legal expenses of getting the will overturned or the trust agreement broken. (They reached quick agreement that family funds should be used to usurp the edicts of Mom and/or Dad.)

In short, it appears unrealistic for parents to expect they reach into the future and manage the priorities of their children, or future generations, *based upon documents developed privately* with legal counsel.

A well-known and respected leader of a Midwestern family drew up plans for the allocation of the family's multi-billion dollar trust-based holdings. As part of the plan, the family-designated Trustee made roughly proportionate reallocations among the trusts of his 11 older children and nieces and nephews. However, for his daughter and son who had not yet reached age 21, he made a different allocation in *structure and amount* for the two younger children.

Unwilling to provide an explanation to his daughter when she realized she had been treated *differently*, the daughter retained council at age 18.   Joined by her then 20 year old brother, they filed a $1 billion lawsuit claiming their father had improperly "raided" her trust fund. They sought to force communication and restoration. The two children also sought $5 billion in punitive damages.   The daughter, reputed to be worth $160 million, was quoted saying, "*..this is not about cash... I just need to know what happened..*"

As part of the legal discovery process, filings were made in court that revealed hitherto undisclosed facts concerning the family's overall financial structure and their use of trusts. The IRS became very interested in the disclosures and the very real possibility of liquidation to meet an additional tax bill (for the family estate) of several billion dollars became a threat to all in the family.

The most useful mechanism for the upcoming generation to carry on the estate in accordance with parental/family values seemed to be to *involve the family fully* in the decision-making process *prior to the transition.*

While great authority is held by a patriarch or matriarch of a family who currently owns/controls the family holdings, it proved naïve to believe the parental authority could be *dependably projected into the future.* Accordingly, for parents to make unilateral decisions regarding the heirs and the transitioning of the estate is neither effective nor unifying.

The "Input" vs. "Control" Issue

Even though our research suggests that successful parents "accept the input of the heirs" in their estate planning decisions that did not necessarily mean yielding parental decision making authority or responsibility. It did mean giving information to heirs, allowing heirs input and influence upon major transition decisions and for heirs input to be received with respect and consideration. The parents sought opportunities in the planning process to invite their heirs to participate. The points in the process where the participation of the heirs was often most welcome arose frequently around shared philanthropic goals. The easiest and most mutually agreed upon situation involved "helping others" and "supporting values in which we (all) believe." And that pointed directly towards the use of philanthropy. A word of caution: This did *not* mean that a family ever saw the primary purpose of philanthropy was to serve as a tool to develop and prepare heirs. However, it is now clear that an *unknown and additional benefit from philanthropy is its use as a tool for preparing heirs.*

A process that integrates the decisions made by the entire family (pre-death) requires that *all* the elements of the estate plan be addressed. Capturing the family's wishes and incorporating them into legal documents is readily done by professionals in the estate planning field. Less obvious is the more-difficult-to-document methods that might be used to achieve the objective of a consensus on the "Family Wealth Mission." And, following a strategy and structure session around the question: "How do we achieve the mission for the family's wealth?", raises the question of who does what? What roles need to be filled, who (from the family) is best suited for each role, who wants to take on a particular role, and how do they develop the required competence to fill that necessary role? These questions seemed to be outside the skill set of most estate planning professionals.

In short, there needs to be an overarching, proven process that engages the entire family, keeps everyone on target, and translates their consensus wishes into specific estate planning instructions. While competent family coaching can provide the "overarching process," one element that offers a continuity of experience for heirs is their involvement and concern with the family philanthropy. Here, philanthropy's importance for the heir is as a teaching, and practice tool… applying family (personal) values on a continuing basis.

With family philanthropies we studied, those with a continuing focus on "mission" provided the heir with some of her/his earliest experiences handling goals, objectives, and targets. Clearly defined philanthropies proved most effective in this lesson. It is not surprising that many recipients of philanthropy attracted funding with simple *mission-oriented names* such as "Save the Whales" and "Cat Action Treasury" and "People for the Ethical Treatment of Animals."

Teaching and practicing the required skills turned out to be much more important than any of the researchers had forecast. Successful families understood what was required of their heirs (with respect to certain skills) and required that those skills be practiced, used and demonstrated within the family environment. In short, the patriarch or matriarch understood that simply "knowing" the right steps was a far cry from "doing" the right steps, i.e., dancing.

Almost like an old Arthur Murray dance studio, the dance steps are painted on the floor, and everyone might agree those walking through those painted steps accurately depicted a waltz …but actually waltzing with another person is an entirely different task. In successful post-transition families, as part of the pre-transition planning the family leaders understood that waltzing knowledge led to waltzing skill *only with actual waltzing practice.* Practice is the point in the learning process where knowledge and skill are integrated and applied. Just because some toes inevitably get stepped on, that is not a reason to discontinue learning how to "dance" together.

Why Do Estates Fail During Post-Transition?

The most important single issue that undermines successful transfers of wealth is the breakdown of trust and communication within the post-transition family unit. This lead back to pre-transition planning. Clearly it failed to prepare the heirs for their responsibilities. These two elements (breakdown of trust and communication, and failure to prepare heirs) combine to cause 85% of the failures of post-transition plans. In fact, less than 3% of the failures were due to professional errors in accounting, legal, or financial advisory planning, leading to higher taxes.

Professionals are generally very good at what they are trained to accomplish. But most families paying for their important advice on financial matters develop a false sense of their own internal readiness for transition. While tax, legal, and financial planning are essential, they are not the complete answer to achieving success in estate transitions.

Of every 1,000 estates that were observed in transition, 700 failed. Of the 700 that failed, 420 (60%) failed due to a *breakdown of trust and communication within the family*. A consequential *failure to prepare the heirs for responsibility* was the cause for another 175 failures, and only 105 failed for *all other causes (including only 20 who failed due to professional oversight or error).* The following diagram illustrates:

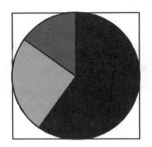

■ **Trust & Communication
Breakdown 60%**

▨ **Failure to Prepare Heirs 25%**

■ **All Other Causes (Tax, Legal,
Mission, etc.) 15%**

different meanings for different families. To interview the 3,250 families we found it necessary to define for each family, precisely what we meant by the words. Without a shared definition of the term, the answers a family provided would not be useful as a basis for conclusions.

As used in our research, the word **"trust"** did not refer to fraud, dishonesty, purposeful deceit or illegal activity[21]. "Trust" was defined as whether or not these *three major components coexist* within individual family relationships:

1. **Reliability,** meaning family members actually *do what they say they will do,* when they promised to do it.

2. **Sincerity,** meaning that the individual's internal (mental) makeup matches his/her external behavior. Family members *mean* what they say.

---

[21] p36, *"Preparing Heirs"*, Williams & Preisser, RDR Publishers, ©2003

3. **Competence,** meaning that the family member has the *skill and capacity* to meet his/her commitments.

All 3 components are required, as well as the presence of an atmosphere of "caring," for authentic trust between individuals. Authentic trust (in the presence of caring) enables individuals to accept the risk of betrayal or failure, knowing that the breach of trust was not intentional, and that efforts will be made to repair the breach.

Communication[22] is based upon authentic trust and *the two other critical elements* of **common mission,** and **common values.** Effective communication means being able to speak openly, honestly, and freely concerning information important to other family members. It requires other family members to know the difference between assessments and statements of fact, and to respond accordingly. It is a skill that requires both knowledge *and* practice. It leads to clarity of understanding and perceptions, unifies the family for common action (until then, communication is simply "noise"), and ultimately to shared responsibilities. Unilateral decision-making (by any family member) that is based on information being withheld or "spun" can be interpreted as insincerity and undermine trust within the family.

Heir Preparation: In most families, we observed that the level of effort invested in preparing heirs is much less than the effort invested in preparing assets for transition. In evaluating the

---

[22] Ibid, p 41

preparedness[23] of the heir(s), we examined issues such as the clarity of mission for the family wealth, and whether or not that mission (and the roles necessary to carry out the strategy for attaining the mission) *is similarly understood by all family members.* Whether or not heirs understand the concepts of accountability, and are provided with early learning opportunities and longer term mentoring, has proven important to the development of self-esteem and effectiveness of the heir. The heirs' self esteem also impacts generational harmony.

Mission of the Family Wealth: This is not the mission of the family or of the family business, but the long term *purpose* of the family's wealth. Without consensus on the purpose[24] of the family's wealth there will be, by default, a variety of interpretations as to priorities. Some members will believe the purpose of the family's wealth is to improve their standard of living; others to preserve, invest, and grow further; some family members will see the purpose as financing education or self-improvement; and others for the purpose of doing "good" and "helping others less fortunate." Varying interpretations, combined with unclear communication and lack of trust creates family disharmony and conflict. Family consensus on a wealth mission saves cost and time by enabling professional advisors to

---

[23] Ibid, p 112, Heir Readiness Checklist
[24] Ibid, p 58

4

respond efficiently (and quickly) to changes in family circumstances. The wealth mission needs to be in writing, and changed only with full family consensus.

Three Focal Points: Philanthropy & Heirs

Therefore, among the most important components of preparing for post-transition success, three components seemed to be routinely linked to philanthropy, specifically family philanthropy[25]. Those three major components are:

1. **VALUES** How did successful pre-transition families reinforce the critical family values that they held dear? Finding a way to do that unified the family over the long term, including the post-transition period after the parents were gone. Those shared and strongly held values were identified, repeated, and reinforced in their heirs from an early age. In view of the fact that family philanthropic activity was unilateral (I will give, or I will not give), the parents continually asked their child *"How does your gift fit with what YOU believe?* And then the family listened carefully and respectfully.

2. **MISSION** What were the tactics that successful pre-transition families used to integrate the concepts of *mission in*

---

[25] Family philanthropy, throughout this book, includes family foundation(s), contributions to charitable tax-exempt foundations, and donor advised fund contributions.

support of the *family philanthropies?*
Again and again the parents used their
family philanthropy and the involvement
of the heir to answer the question "Just
what is it you (the donor) and they (the
donee) are trying to accomplish?" "Is it a
good fit with our family's mission?"

3. **ACCOUNTABILITY** How did families
use their mission and values to evaluate
the effectiveness of their contributions? It
was clear that, for successful families, the
combination of family values and agreed
upon mission would inevitably lead to the
family leaders asking the question of both
the donor (heir) and the donee: "Did it
happen as forecast?" "Did they do what
they said they'd do with your donation?"

Each of the following chapters focuses upon one
of the 5 major "Developmental Stages" (age
brackets) defined by researchers such as
Erickson, Piaget, Havinghurst, and the Drake
University Department of Developmental
Psychology. Although often written in the
present tense, it is condensed from what
successful post-transition families told us (and
demonstrated to us) was being done (or had been
done) to use philanthropy as a tool for preparing
their heirs. The most persuasive lesson, that of
experience, comes through clearly. It works!

Chapter 5

Age 5 to 10, The Awakening Years

Discovering One's Personal Influence

Prior to this time, the child/heir has been, for the most part, a "managed member of the family." By that we mean that the imposition of parental will has been almost total. Aside from the occasional tantrum, or outburst of crying, or fighting with siblings, the daily life of the child has been set and controlled by the parents. What to eat, when to go to bed, when to get up, what to wear, the daily/weekly/monthly schedule, travel... all have been set around a larger family routine. Acquisition of language skills, conformance to family routine, and the ultimate authority of parental figures have been modeled and subconsciously absorbed by the child during these first years. In fact, parents have unconsciously modeled their values for the child, and the child has begun acceptance of those parental/family values, usually without either party being aware of its occurrence. Child behaviorists know that as the child approaches the age of 5, if these underpinnings of submission to family and parental authority should be firmly in place. If not, it is not likely that our research findings that led to this book can be effectively applied in those situations.

Thus, age 5 can be viewed as a sort of embarkation point, and beginning of the child's ability to absorb and learn a new set of lessons about the world "outside." In general, this is when the child begins to express interests and ignites the first fires of passion or focused interests. Interest and care for animals. Love of a particular storybook, a favorite playmate, and vocalization of priorities ("I want to do this first", "why can't we do that now...") and the beginning of limitations. "There isn't enough time to do all that..." and "...you can't have every toy in the set" are the beginnings of a sense of limits.

First, the child expresses interests and wants. Then, the parent begins to set boundaries. One result is the child's awareness that while he/she is able to express choice, conflicts do occur and are a routine part of life. Very quickly these conflicts cause the child to seek some sort of a resolution mechanism. The child's resultant question of "can we do it after dinner?" or the "why not, Johnny has all the toys in the set?" are nothing more than the child's observations of "they have" or "they can." It naturally leads to your child asking "why can't I?"

Such requests are simply the child's expression of his/her frustration with limits. *Our research shows that it is important for the child to experience limitations in order to have "unmet desires" as a 'normal' part of life. Without these unmet desires, we have observed repeated cases of troubled heirs in affluent families, and accompanying self-destructive behavior.*[26]

---

[26] While we are not psychologists, this has been observed frequently enough by us that it deserves emphasis.

Because they loved their grandchildren, every time Orville and Diana went on a trip they brought something back for them.

They soon discovered that the grandchildren greeted them with the question: "…what did you bring back for me this trip!??"

Realizing that the grandchildren were beginning to equate love and remembrance with gifts of "things," Orville and Diana promptly discontinued the practice. The grandchildren, disappointed at first, quickly adjusted to the return of Grandpa and Grandma as the "most important event" of their trip… not gifts.

In general, the opportunities for the 5-10 year old age bracket are opportunities for "stage setting" in the three major areas that philanthropy *can* affect, and that are also important to ultimate post (estate) transition success…Values, Mission, and Accountability. In general, successful post-transition families seemed to have "begun to set the stage" for their young heirs centered around the following framework:

"THE BIG PICTURE" – AGES 5-10

VALUES: Remind them that they chose their friends because they *liked them*, not because they have *things*. Fun things do not make fun people. Share their interests and encourage them. Accept as valid their passionate concerns. Introduce the concept of proportionality in allowance expenditures.. how *much* of their allowance should go to any one item.

MISSION: Continually ask the child "what the action or wish leads to", and what his/her *overall hope (plan)* is for collecting an "entire set" or "the complete collection." To what end? For what purpose? Try to link acting on the wish to an ultimate outcome...and discuss how to attain the child's desired outcome.

ACCOUNTABILITY: Follow up on decisions and actions taken by the child in exercise of their personal will. Ask if they "got what they hoped for" and "if you did it again, what would you do differently?" "Were there surprises in the purchase?" "Where are the items at this very moment?" "Are they cared for?" "Did that friend do what he/she promised?"

VALUES - Building Opportunities-Age 5 to 10

Here it becomes important to listen carefully to discover what really matters to the child. *It is a mistake simply to try to impose your values upon the child.* The goal here is simply to have the children *declare their passion.* For them to feel you care, and for the parent to listen while the child begins to talk about his/her passion, maintains a critically open door for communication.

The concept of "Values" is abstract to your child, and children mature at wildly different rates during this period. The concept may begin to be discussable at age 5, or not until age 10. It is their first expression of what they begin to *care about*, beyond their personal needs (food, play, sleep, etc.) The tiniest spark can, over time, grow into a realization that "action can be taken on my passion... and that's a good thing." It is not critically important what the passion may be. The child should not be "educated" by the parent as to why their passion may be "wrong."

For instance, they may become passionate about saving all lost small animals. This is not the time to explain that humane societies often have to put animals to death because of the inability to "adopt out" all unwanted animals that are turned over to them... or because of the danger to children of uncared for animals running "wild" about the community streets, etc. This is the time to support their passion, and to compliment them on their *caring for others*. This is the opportunity to open the door to helping the child to save part of his/her allowance to buy food for the animal shelter. In short, it is time to validate their passion (if not the object of that passion), the caring, and the concern for others in any form. These passions and concerns and sensitivities form the foundation of caring for other family members, of learning to take action on one's passions, and to know they can be discussed with Mom and Dad.

Tom's parents had never gone to school beyond the 6th grade, and were blue-collar workers. Both parents were concerned about Tom's future. In 1948, they asked the Principal of Tom's elementary school in Santa Monica, California: *"..based on your years of experience, can you give us guidelines we could follow so our son grows up to be a good boy?"*

The Principal, Mr. Sparks, thought and then replied: *"I am certain of two rules in my 26 years as an elementary school principal. First, never permit him to be cruel to animals, and, second, allow him to read anything he wants, from comic books to pulp fiction."* The Principal explained to the somewhat surprised parents: *"If he learns to be kind to animals, he will automatically be kind to people... and if he experiences joy in reading, he will always enjoy learning."*

Tom read virtually every comic book, paperback novel, and newspaper he could get his hands on, and never even squished a bug. He became passionate about philanthropy, went on with his education, completing his PhD. Now married and successfully parenting two competent children of his own... they too are growing up under Principal Sparks' two rules.

Allowance: This is the appropriate time to introduce allowance and set some guidelines on its use. Not as payment for "chores." Chores are simply the admission ticket to be part of the family and carry part of the workload in the household. Some well-known families, early on, set the "1/3, 1/3, 1/3 rule." Saving 1/3 of one's allowance was a "standard" for receiving an allowance. Spending 1/3 on one's self was acceptable as long as the final 1/3 was spent for the benefit of some other deserving cause[27]. Of course, the term "deserving cause" took some explaining from time to time, but the parent continued to listen respectfully, never belittling the cause. Successful post-transition families did *not* define the "deserving causes." They simply asked the child to *have some standards of their own in order to identify what was 'deserving.'*

Note what the families did: they set an early standard *as a condition of receiving one's first allowance.* It was not simply the commencement of the allowance. The hidden messages embedded in this rule were summarized by:

- Never spend more than you receive, or even spend all that you receive... for them, that was a family value they wanted taught early on.

- Consider others to be as valuable as you consider yourself. That doesn't mean you are diminished or reduced, it means that you are respectful of the needs of the world you live in.

- By discussing and measuring how well you *follow* the "1/3 rule" you will learn *accountability.*

- Money is a tool, and how that tool is used can impact others in an important way. How do you determine *what* you wish to impact/help, and *how do you hold others accountable?*

---

[27] This rule was set by one of America's wealthiest families before the advent of income taxes, charitable deductions, or the appearance of the public relations profession.

Each time the allowance is given to the child (weekly for the 5-10 year old age bracket), it is worthwhile to do the following:

- Let your child know how much money has been saved and praise him/her for it (accountability, reserve for the future).

- Ask your child what he/she did with the next 1/3 of the allowance, and whether or not they would "spend it again" in the same way (post assessment, accountability, value)

- Discuss with your child what the plans are for giving away the final 1/3. What cause is it likely to go for, when, and what specific actions will they take to see that their hopes (for the money) are realized? (mission, values, forward thinking, anticipation of results, preparation for accountability in others)

These conversations are probably worth 5 to 10 minutes time. Avoid lengthy conversations. Don't lecture. Give your child the experience of being listened to. Seek to become involved with your child's thinking and priorities. Help with thinking through *how* to go about accomplishing the tasks facing the child. Help your child set expectations of others with whom he/she is likely to become involved - the charity, the "banker" (holder of the savings to date and the monies to be contributed). Involvement and comfortable conversations about the use of money are the goals of the parental involvement.

Eric was concerned that his young son and daughter were being caught up with material wants due to the advertising, friends, and trips to the mall. Their bedrooms were stocked with toys, stuffed animals, and games. Eric and his wife were concerned that their children's possessions were becoming valued less, as "new" became more important.

One evening, over dinner, they worked out a mutually agreeable solution with their children:

For every new toy, stuffed animal or game, they would choose a similar possession to give away before the new possession could enter the house. The children were free to choose the beneficiary such as the Thrift Store, Women's Shelter, etc.

This solution pleased everyone; set limits on the value attached to the *number of possessions,* and added the experience of giving away possessions not in daily use.

A SPECIFIC EXERCISE

Allowing young children to give to their church/temple/mosque, or to scouting, their sport team or school gave an interesting opportunity to several families After the child had given a few times, they encouraged the child to ask the pastor, scout leader; "How do you keep track of the contributions? Do you keep a ledger to record expenses and gifts?" This did several things. It set a standard for the child of "when you give money, *someone* needs to follow up to see if the money went where it was supposed to go," and that they too can expect someone to ask *them* to be accountable for the assets they control.

Mission Defining Opportunities - Age 5 to 10

During these early years children make continuing assumptions about *why* their parents do what they do. Children are brought along on tasks because it's a way to keep them cared for... within reach. Often they are in the car or at the store with absolutely no sense of why they are along, or why Mom/Dad is going to the store or to the grandparent's home. This is the time to set the stage for the importance of *Mission*. The concept to be planted is that of the simplest of sentences:

> *"If you haven't agreed upon a destination, directions and time tables aren't very relevant."*

This period is important because it offers a parent the opportunity to inject a sense of purpose into the heir's thinking. With a sense of purpose, or reason, questioning and communication can take place. In the families we studied, this encouragement to question did not generate ceaseless wrangling over purpose. To the contrary, it seemed to encourage participation and involvement of the children in the preparatory activities of the parents.

In the family philanthropies studied, the concepts of mission and goals were established early on and related to practical daily/weekly events that could easily be tracked. In one instance of explaining the concept of mission in terms of destination, the parent would drive the child to the store, school, ball game, etc, causing the child to ask "where are we going?" Sometimes the parent would pretend to take the child to the store when the child knew they are supposed to be going to school. The children asked why they were not going to school as planned. This proved to be a good moment for the parent to thank the child for reminding them of their goal, their destination... and point out now is the time to take corrective action. Yes, a little far-fetched, but it worked.

Accountability Applying Opportunities - Age 5 to 10

Accountability for this age group is *not* about "meeting a standard" or "punishment for failure." That sort of accountability drove children *away* from communication and participation. The successful families saw accountability (for this age group) as more of *achievement of the child's personal objective*. Frequently it was related to allowance usage issues. Specifically, the family gradually moved away from holding the child accountable for the personal use of *"their disposable 1/3."* Whether the personal funds went for candy, music CDs, Care Bear toys, or "I don't remembers", the parents made light of the outcome. However, on the (frequently matched) "saving 1/3," and for the "give away 1/3" the parents explained that they felt entitled to discuss mission or targets/goals because the money of others was involved. Besides, promises had been made by the child to the parents and from the parents to the child.

"Allowance will be \$7/week[28] and it will be paid Friday evening at dinner." In turn, the parents asked that the savings and charitable "balances available" be posted on the child's bedroom wall so they can see how the family money is accumulating. This made it easy for the family to encourage expanded vision, or expanded mission for the charitable component as the funds accumulated. It also seemed to be a stimulant to action, because funds just building up weren't accomplishing anything. Often the two "accumulator accounts" were conversationally "linked" by the parents, e.g., "Well I can see you are getting enough saved for that new bike you want, but what are you going to do with your charitable savings when you get that bike?" "Have you thought about that?" "Maybe you can ride your bike down to the Humane Society and make your donation that same day you buy your bike? That would be a fun ride!"

Finally, the notion of accountability needs to include *parental failure to perform*. Successful families always added *their own penalty* for

---

[28] One rule of thumb for allowance was \$1 per week for each year of age. The variable occurred depending upon how it was to be used. For a 9 year old 3rd grader, \$9/week is about right if they are saving 1/3, spending 1/3, and giving away 1/3....providing they aren't required to do anything with their portion such as purchasing their own clothes, pay for their movies, etc. For older children, allowances increased based upon the parent's expectations as to how it was to be used for personal expenses... and then worked backward to attain the 1/3, 1/3, 1/3 balance.

Mom/Dad failing to perform... which the child responded to with some glee. For example Mom might say: "And if we forget to pay your allowance by 5pm Friday, we will pay you an additional 20% penalty... but not if you fail to call it to our attention." Or, "We will match your savings account AND your charitable account on a dollar-for-dollar basis. And, if we fail to do so, and you call it to our attention, we will double the match for each week we've missed." This enabled the families to learn the concept of cross-accountability. It also moved the discussion of money matters to a more equal footing, and taught the child/heir the value of accountability for all. Talking about the charitable accumulation and/or the personal savings accounts (and the parental match) made conversations surrounding both money *and* accountability normal, easy, and allowed it to take place in a non-charged atmosphere for all. A valuable lesson.

Chapter 6

Age 11 to 15, The Exploring Years

Discovering self in the midst of change

During this period the child is experiencing dramatic changes in their emotional and social world.   It is a period of turmoil as they pass from childhood to young adulthood.   He/she begins consciously to seek out (and be influenced by) others beyond their family.   Leaving behind a period of steady and predictable physical growth, playmates, bicycles, family events and family friends, the child begins to expand his/her social awareness.

This can be the single most emotionally challenging period in your child's life.   Often referred to as (passage through) "the middle school years," the child becomes aware that life and happiness *do* seem to depend upon her/him. This is a somewhat startling discovery, that one can affect one's life... for better or worse.   This simple concept: "I impact my life" has sometimes overwhelming implications for one who has not learned how to control "impact."   The child is beginning to ask the question of "who am I to my family and in the world?"... and beginning to expect a bigger answer than "..a good girl/boy."

It is in this emotional period following the awakening years that the child begins to explore *how* they affect the world they live in without a clear understanding of cause and effect.   It is wildly confusing.   They learn how to attract the attention of another.   They learn which social group they would like to be a part of (for good reasons or bad) and how to behave to enter that group. They cope with their own personal failures to socialize or win the hearts and minds of their new interests and friends. One day they are immune to harshest criticism, and the next day they are absolutely crushed by the mildest rebuke. As one counselor of early teens said: *"All* kids that age are on *mood-altering drugs...* drugs called estrogen and testosterone!"

Peers play an increasingly important role throughout this period. The notion of "friend" and "enemy" loom larger than life itself. This is a period of learning to cope (however ineptly) with rejection and disappointment. That rejection and disappointment is based partially upon their own actions and perceptions, and partially upon the actions and circumstances of others. It is this unfamiliarity with the needs of other similar-age schoolmates that is so puzzling to the middle-schooler. They blame themselves for everything that "goes wrong." They cannot imagine that their schoolmates are also going through the same self-blaming. Relationship concepts like a "natural fit" or "synchronicity between beings" are not in their vocabulary or their comprehension.

This emotional whirlpool is, in the judgment of the families we interviewed, perhaps the *least productive time for concepts such as family values, family mission, and accountability.*

Scott and Mary Ellen were concerned about improving communication within their own family. They noted that their church was involved in a 3rd world church-building program. They invited their oldest child, on his 13th birthday, to join dad on a jungle safari to build a church.

The 2 weeks father and son spent together living in the jungle with other members of their church and youth group, building the simplest of structures for another culture, also built strong communication bonds. The experience was so powerful that Scott took the sons, and Mary Ellen took the daughters when they each reached their 13th birthday. The children who had previously been on the trip helped parents prepare the siblings for "their trip."

It brought an entirely new level of vocabulary and communication to the family, and became an enduring and cherished event in their memories.

Not giving up during this period is hard work for parents. Young people are *so* distracted, and in such emotional turmoil during this period that they seem to be immune to learning anything outside not relevant to their immediate social concerns. Parents, at the same time, enter a period of intense empathy for their children, and find themselves "hurting for their child." Parents seek ways to help ease the pain of social learning, schoolmate associations, physical changes, awkwardness, and fumbling the handling of new situations. Realizing that such buffering of their child's pain is impossible, parents of successful post-transitions suffered through this period and worked to keep communication alive. One of the tools used by families was to help the child's self esteem with alternative rewarding involvements. Family philanthropy offered them that opportunity.

Dependable Islands of Constancy

Very few elements of a child's life *carry through* from childhood into adolescence. Those elements that do offer the child a sense of security are a great aid. During this exploring period of social relationships, with widely differing rates of maturing, family, pets, and the physical home site are major elements of constancy. Kids may come home crying, but they come home. They now cry privately, in the presence of an individual family member, where they can expect to be heard and comforted. Meals together are great stabilizers. Travel together as a family offers a new environment and often fresh starts at new social encounters. Their pets, and their pet causes become welcome refuges in a time of change. One of the major opportunities for carry through is the continuation of the child's "heart" issues.

Charitable or philanthropic causes often can blossom at this age… sometimes because they are a refuge from uncertainty of middle school issues. Sometimes because a new level of insight emerges. And, occasionally, a new "cause" emerges for the child as a result of a shared interest with another child. Often the "new cause" can emerge as part of schoolwork or reading or an entertainment program such as those carried by The Discovery Channel or National Geographic Channel. Schoolwork is focused upon widening horizons, increasing awareness of the world we live in, and presenting old thoughts and ideas to new minds ready to learn them. *Whatever the origin, a sense of continuity and stability can be fed, and reinforced, through the use of philanthropy.*

Near the end of the middle school period, around age 14-15, you can expect the child's philanthropic interests to begin to converge into a few long-term interests. There will be other causes and other charities that appeal to the adult persona of your child, but the general empathies developed at this age seem to continue over the years. This is the equivalent of their "childhood (charitable) sweetheart" that is never forgotten, and thought of warmly over the years to come. It is always welcomed back into their lives after periods of absence, eagerly conversed with, and a comfortable friend until the end of one's life.

At this time in their lives, the child becomes more thoughtful and learns not simply to accept the values of others with respect to the child's philanthropic or charitable interests. It is becoming increasingly difficult to change his/her interests substantially.

"THE BIG PICTURE" – AGE 11 to 15

VALUES: Good time to remind the child of the importance of their *constancy* and *reliability* to the charity they support. Discuss why they believe in the charity itself, or do they believe in the objective of the charity? Talk about what charitable organization seems to most closely match with the values of the child and family.
MISSION: Follow up with conversations examining those philanthropies wishing to *improve* the situation, versus those wishing to *preserve* the situation. Which is the appropriate point of view? Can you support the charity's long-term mission?
ACCOUNTABILITY: This is a good time to introduce the concept of what institution or charity might *best* deliver assistance to the child's charity of choice. Ask how the child plans to follow the charity once high school and college enter the picture.

Talk with your child about her/his philanthropy and you will easily detect the maturation of interest and values, and will realize that substantial progress has evolved.

In general, the opportunities for the 11-15 year old age bracket are opportunities for "stage consolidation in a social setting" for the three major areas that philanthropy *can* affect. Those same areas are critical to ultimate post (estate) transition success...*Values, Mission, and Accountability.* In general, successful post-transition families seem to have "begun to set the stage" for their young heirs by practicing the following:

Family Values Strengthening Opportunities - Age 11 to 15

During this period, philanthropic involvement offers several opportunities for *stabilizing* the child during a normally turbulent time. Pursuit of the philanthropic interest for the child offers increasingly complex opportunities for involvement. Expect the child to become aware of the social benefits of a shared interest in a particular philanthropy.

The concern for the environment attracts many younger people because it is eminently understandable as a good cause. Participation in a band, a sports team, even supporting a fund-raising group to pay for transportation to an "away" game will provide the heir with team and teamwork experiences. A concern for the homeless, or those who are disabled, often gathers a corps of passionate advocates, especially if the child's family has a "special needs" member. Endangered species (especially the more recognizable ones such as elephants, cats, gorillas, and dolphins) is another passion that is often a bridge to the interests of other schoolmates. Philanthropy is one of the consistent opportunities to "build bridges" to other individuals and groups in an otherwise confusing period.

As parents, those who were successful in helping their child grow worked hard to be nonjudgmental as their child "switched passions" from one cause to another. No sooner had the child embraced dolphins than she discovered the cutest boy in the class was doing a science project on Cheetahs. That day she came home with Cheetah books from the library and began looking at cat-based philanthropies. Here it becomes important to help the child ride through the emotional and social storms of the Middle-School years. Philanthropy can be one of the very few "constants" in the too-rapidly evolving life of a young person. There are many opportunities for parents to make use of it in a constructive role. It is worthwhile to remind your child in casual conversations that the *recipients of philanthropy* rely upon the constancy and steadiness of the philanthropist.

Encourage your child to invite other children to charitable settings and fund-raisers, visits to the charitable offices, and field trips to observe the application of the charitable funds. Other parents are routinely supportive of such outings and long-term stable friendships emerge.

Parents and children can be sensitive to (and gather) public information surrounding the *child's* philanthropy of choice. This is a time when children can begin to absorb and comprehend what others think of the charitable work being accomplished. It reinforces their personal values.

It is important for your child to know that you are aware of what is happening with her/his charity. It is important for the child to hear that you respect what is being accomplished, and for the child to be recognized (and publicly praised) in front of others.

Honore routinely saved her charitable money for preservation of the Panda. It reminded her of the "Care Bears" she had on her bedroom comforter. She became a regular contributor to the World Wildlife Foundation (whose symbol is the Panda) via the local zoo, where her grandmother was a Docent.

In the 6th grade, students had to complete a group science project. Assigned to a group, Honore and the other girl decided on Pandas while the 2 boys decided on Tigers. The teacher came over to the group to find out why they hadn't compromised, and encouraged the group to work on something closer to home. He asked the group *"How does our local Humane Society handle **wild** animals brought to its doorstep?"*

Absorbed in this group science project, the group became close friends. Next year, Honore shifted her charitable support from WWF to the local Humane Society...where today she and one of her 6th grade science project teammates serve on its Board.

The dinner table, gatherings with other family members, and peer families with similarly (charitably) involved children are good opportunities for reinforcement of the value of *reliability*. Comments in public concerning the child's interests and contribution of time to areas of passion indicate to your child that you value his/her choices and actions. It is a powerful reinforcement of the value of caring beyond one's self. Later in life such actions can support feelings of caring for elders in the family, sensitivity toward those who work in the family home or office, and respect for the contributions that others make in simply making life move ahead.

A parent in a wealthy community noticed that his child and a neighbor's child had set up a lemonade stand at the curb to raise money for their scout troop. Pleased with this "spirit of entrepreneurship," he strolled over to congratulate the children. He noticed *two different prices* for lemonade posted on the stand: "50 cents a glass/5 cent a glass" Imagining some sort of "quantity discount" he asked "Why the two prices?" The children happily responded by answering: "Well, the people in our neighborhood can afford to pay 50 cents, but for people outside our neighborhood, 50 cents is too much." From "Preparing Heirs", ©2003, www.thewilliamsgroup.org

---

As mentioned earlier, one of the major values that create a unified family over the long terms is the value of authentic *trust*[29]. Do not underestimate how closely your child is paying attention to what you say and do as parents. You cannot "hate the Smiths" in private and then "be charming to the Smiths" in public. Children

---

[29] Recall that *authentic trust*, common mission, and common values are the 3 requirements for family or team unity over the long term. Our research clearly shows that if *any one* of these 3 components is missing, the family or team will not remain coherent over the long-term. Transactional trust (simply based on competence, reliability, and sincerity) requires the additional component of *caring* in order to become *authentic trust*.

will question this face-switching behavior and doubt your praise for their own philanthropic interest. They will question your sincerity, and begin to define parental behavior as a "cordial hypocrisy" that shifts with the winds of social need. If you are not consistent in other behaviors, the child will come to doubt any behavior you show toward their interests, including the child's (passionate) philanthropy of choice.

Mission Defining Opportunities - Age 11 to 15

This is the time when you begin to integrate the child into the concept of "we support your mission." This is meant to affirm and embrace the child's sense of mission, i.e. "what I'd like to accomplish with my involvement in this cause." This means that the child can, and should, understand that the family charity, the family foundation, believes that the child's cause is also worthy of consideration as the family's own (shared) cause. It is a step toward removing the barrier between what the family spends on its philanthropy, and what the child spends on his/her own philanthropy.

The concept of "mission" is not new to the child, although the word itself may be unfamiliar. The term "mission" or "goal" is sometimes difficult for a young person to internalize. Families found it helpful to use sport "goals" like soccer, football, basketball, etc. The key to developing a mission in cooperation with the young person will be the long-term purpose, goal or mission *he/she strives for* as a result of his/her philanthropic gifts. Mission examples may be helping the poor, helping other kids with physical or mental challenges, helping the environment—these are all good goals and missions to which most children readily relate.

Mission is present in such concepts as "winning the league soccer championship" and "saving up to buy a 'Mongo-Brand' skateboard" and "reading 12 books by the end of the school year."

Additionally, the concept of the family involvement and support of the child's mission proved to be an important and helpful experience in the families we studied. Families often considered broadening the mission of the family philanthropy to include the child's charitable mission. The following steps are synthesized from families who acted to make this inclusive transition:

- Declare, at a family meeting, that you (the parent) have become increasingly aware of the importance of the child's mission and the child's unwavering support of that mission. Recite what you believe the mission to be (thus demonstrating understanding and appreciation of the child's target charity).

- Make a statement that the family would like to match the child's financial support for the child's mission/charity. State a specific amount (100% match seemed to be most frequently used) and a time that support can commence.

- Seek approval from the entire family, whether or not they are formally members of a family foundation[30]. This was critically important. It recognized maturity of interest, worthiness of cause, and set expectations for the other children/heirs concerning their ability to seek and receive support for their "passions."

- Recite, before all family members, the family philanthropy's "mechanism for action."

- The family will ask the child to fill out a check drawn on the family's philanthropy account matching the child's contribution.

- The family member who is a signator on that family philanthropy account will sign the check.

- The child will personally deliver the check to the intended charity, along with his own contribution, returning with a receipt.

- The child will report back semi-annually on "how things are going" with the designated charity

One tool we observed to be effective is the concept of **"energy."** Heirs-in-waiting can invest **energy** by working at a soup kitchen, an orphanage, hospital (children's) or Habitat for Humanity, Katalysis (Women's Village Banking in Central America); World Vision; enabling them to see money as **"stored energy"**.

---

[30] Family Foundations were often quite modest in size, yet very effective in their learning power for the heirs. Many family foundations we saw were less than $50,000 in total endowment. Size did not seem to have impact on learning.

Accountability Applying Opportunities - Age 11 to 15

This is when parents begin to feel comfortable that the earlier lessons are beginning to show signs of real worth. Education around the concept of accountability seems to have been the easiest for our study families. Work and family

---

Susan's sister had been a special needs child since her birth. To deepen the family's sense of mission (beyond sending a check to the Mentally Handicapped Association) Susan persuaded her entire family to participate in the "Flowers of Hope" annual campaign.

For one weekend the family of 6 participated with other families in measuring flower seeds into packets, and mailing them out with information packets about the charity's goals.

It became an annual event for Susan's family, where even the youngest members of the family learned values, and the joy of direct participation.

---

lives were closely tied to accountability. The bottom line in their business life, the performance of their financial assets, the met (and unmet) expectations in their personal relationships. Everyone is involved in assessments of one sort or another, consciously measuring one's self against some standard; parents, colleagues, the numbers of the year before completing college, the way I feel after a night of partying vs. the way I feel when I don't party, etc. Introducing a sense of accountability to heirs-in-waiting seems to have come easy to families we researched.

The major difference between successful and unsuccessful families was their "touch." By that difficult-to-define word, we refer to whether or not the family leader seemed to be heavy handed... unilaterally imposing their (parental) accountability standards with the threat of "cutoff" if not met, and an implication of "I'll step in and take over if things are not going well." The successful families seemed to have a much greater sense of proportion, and a lighter "touch" when introducing this concept to their children.

The amount of money that was being tracked and accounted for was relatively small (a percentage of the child's allowance or accumulated earnings). However, the lessons to be learned were important. The lessons to be learned were judged to be much more valuable than any "wasted" money. In fact, successful families expected the child to make mistakes and to be forgetful. When that happened, the money "wasted" was seen as "tuition due" for the learning experience that resulted. Most families were pleasantly surprised by how careful the heir became once the "family money" was involved. They were often surprised by the criteria applied by the child, and the actions taken by the child when the charity fell short of the child's expectations (read: values).

Another frequently used tool by successful families was expressed in their belief that "What you learn in school can be applied to your favorite charity." Most parents ask the vague and general question: "What did you learn in school today?" or "How did things go today at school?" Our experience is that middle-schooler's answers match the vagueness of the question. Virtually no information (of use) is exchanged following a vague question. Often, the child responds to a more specific question such as "...in your math class, did you figure out yet how to calculate the average cost per tiger saved" or " ...have you figured out yet how to look up the percentage of your contribution that actually goes to help the children in Haiti?"

Specific questions require specific answers, and also serve the secondary purpose of alerting the child to practical applications of what is being presented in the classroom. If the answer is a simple "No" from the child, it offers the opportunity to ask "...what are you learning that *might* help you with that humane society project?" *"How do you research* that question? Do you have *access* to encyclopedias, or are you *learning to use* the Internet?" Those questions, when asked, model the parental value of accountability. And, at this age, parental modeling is still a powerful tool, although peer group pressure will soon become dominant.

Several successful foundation families encouraged their heirs-in-waiting to ask the pastor, rabbi, or scout leader for information regarding their giving. Such questions helped the children seek accountability in others as they sought to discover if their donation went where it was supposed to go.

The Sorenson family had decided that their five children should each be responsible for giving $1,000 to a charity of their choice. Each child chose a charity and the 13 year old daughter decided she would give her $1,000 to the Children's Home.

The following year the family met again to decide on their charitable grants. When the now 14 year old daughter was asked if she was going to give to the Children's Home again, she said, "No." She told the family that the Children's Home did not send her a "thank you" note and she had worked at the home several weekends only to learn her money was used to raise more money and did not go directly to the children in the home. This due diligence set the child, and the family on an entirely new track.

Today, 25 years later, all the children are solid decision makers, performing due diligence on everything they do. They manage the family foundation, and have done so for many years. Their grants are highly effective and the families' values are continually reinforced. Their children have learned how to give, and that money is a tool, not a determinant of who they are as people. ©2003 "Preparing Heirs" p. 107

This empowered the children, and at the same time helped them to understand that they too can expect to be held accountable. The due diligence process in families we studied was guided by Mom and Dad, who participated in asking where/how the funds were spent. Over time children began to learn how to ask respectfully. They also learned how to "dig a little" for further information as they sought to make sure their funds went where directed.

Allowance and Accountability:

This is the time of transition from "less *allowance*, more *reward* for assuming and discharging responsibility." That means linking increases in allowance to performance with respect to schoolwork, homework, household duties, and adherence to household rules concerning home time, phone time, Internet and game time. It is also the time to encourage the child to stick close to his/her own *expenditure* guidelines as to what to do with earnings/allowance. Expect to begin discussing (explaining?) the philosophical underpinnings of why the 1/3 rule was established in the first place. Expect the child to want to pull away and "reset" the rules so they are more flexible, easier to get around, more subject to change.

Successful post-transition families did allow the child to begin exerting influence over changes to the rules, but not *control or final say over the rules*. As long as the child is not a fully supporting adult, it is reasonable for parents to expect that the Golden Rule will be followed: "...the parent (who has the gold) sets the rules." Not unilaterally, and not without discussion. It was clear that the successful families readily made adjustments to the rules as time and experience accumulated. But, parents avoided simply "caving in" on their prior position or allowance policy. The hidden messages that were embedded in this rule were summarized by:

- You can influence the rules, but you cannot control the rules.

- I want your input because you have more experience and knowledge than you had before.

- While the rules may change, and priorities may change, it is not likely that our (family) values will change.

- We still review what's happening with your expenditures because I am interested in what you do, enjoy seeing your growth, and I need to see if our agreement is generally being followed.

It is still worthwhile for successful families to do the following:

- Let your child know how much money is in his/her *savings* account, praise him/her for it (accountability, reserve for the future), and expect questions on when and how it may be used. (expect to hear the argument: "If I can't spend it, what good is it?")

- Discuss with your child, in general terms, what he/she did with the *expenses* 1/3 of the allowance, and whether or not they would "spend it again" in the same way (post assessment, accountability, value)

- Discuss with your child what the *philanthropic* plans are for the final 1/3. This may be a good time to talk about your feelings of supportiveness for their philanthropy. Those feelings of support could mean matching contributions from the

> family's philanthropic support, greatly increasing the impact of the child's savings.

These conversations deserve 15 to 20 minutes time at a session. Avoid lengthy conversations, as those seemed to turn into debates. Find a pleasant way to change the topic so that money conversations do *not* become your most important conversations. Above all, parents are advised not to lecture. You are entering the period where children (unfortunately and incorrectly) assess your intelligence and wisdom as (steadily) diminishing.

This point of view will continue for about another 20 years, and then will reverse polarity. You will then be on the "upswing." Your children will begin to seek your counsel as they begin to cope with their own children and life problems. Until then, there is little you can do about this process except avoid the conflict that comes with differing assessments surrounding the value of *your* involvement. Instead of debating, or trading assessments, view these events as opportunities to give your child the experience of being "listened to." It is rare, both as an adolescent or an adult, that one has the personal experience of someone granting our words and thought "legitimacy"... which can be done whether or not you agree with the speaker. The old maxim of "seek first to understand, and then to be understood" has real value for this age group.

Chapter 7

Age 16 to 20, The Developing Years

Understanding Accountability

During this period the young adult child is moving steadily towards separation. The world of school, friends, teachers, and *requirements* for progress begin to close in around him/her. Changes in their emotional and social world begin to slow, and longer term friendships begin to emerge. Aspects such as mutuality of interest and shared (with friends) obstacles to success begin to become increasingly important.

They have effectively moved into "separateness" and are allowed to further distance themselves from their home routine, their local geography, and parental direction. Brothers and sisters a year or two behind seem more remote and less influential on the quality of the older child's daily life. Access to a car, use of the internet, and periods of absence (including overseas learning and vacations) become part of the High School and College experience. The accessories of physical and personal privacy (dorms, closed doors, automobiles, etc.), with boundaries being defined and set by the child, are major elements of this period. This often fiercely maintained privacy offers the opportunity to experiment with alcohol, drugs, sex, perhaps with funds designated for other purposes. In our research, the desire to "belong" to some group was often influenced by an unstated embarrassment surrounding the financial success of their family, or the widespread recognition of the family name (in that community). Heirs often felt urged to demonstrate their independence by reckless or rebellious behavior, and philanthropy became one of the "firm places" to maintain a foothold while still claiming an identity for themselves.

Kyle was 18, and packing for his fall enrollment at college. Instead, he took the offer to work with a program designed for the poor in Africa. He spent the next year working in a remote location in Africa before returning to college.

His first day back in America required him to "go to the store." He was overwhelmed at the range of choices he faced, and the almost limitless quantity of food. His first reaction, he explained to his family, was one of anger. "That store had more food in it than one village in Africa would see in 10 years!"

He suddenly gained a different appreciation of America's freedom of choices, and the good fortune of his family. As a passionate, informed, and articulate advocate, he persuaded the family to shift its philanthropic focus to international assistance programs (UNESCO, etc.), leading the foundation in a new policy direction.

The decision on which college to apply to, and the beginning of focus on career interests, are the center points of young adult planning. Yet, even those decisions are more strongly influenced by friends and heartthrob than by parents. The major difficulty for parents in this time period is remaining "connected." Forced to accept the increasing personal separateness (and privacy) that is common for this period, ties to the family are stretched and tested. Family and the physical home site are no longer the refuge they once were. Friends, activities built around school (clubs, sports, class work, travel), and the fear of failure become increasingly important during this period.

This is a time when the young adult tries to find their own "balance point" between focus on *requirements*, and focus on *friends*. They become aware that their junior and senior high school *grades*, their SAT *scores*, and their scholastic/sports/leadership *activities* will directly affect their college admittance chances. Their performance in college will dramatically affect their post-college employment or graduate school applications. Reality begins to close in, and the solutions lie all within one's self.

For the first time they have more to study than they can accomplish. Selectivity of *what* to study and *when* to study becomes a more important decision... and one they have to make on their own. They face the choice of going to the party or to the library. It is a period of deciding "how serious do I want to be?" In short, the concept of *accountability* has arrived, only to settle heavily on their developing shoulders.

One of the problems with *accountability* is the irreversibility of certain outcomes. Accountability is simply another way of referring to (some inevitable) consequences, or outcomes. Drinking, then driving can have disastrous consequences, or no consequences. Failing to turn in a final project by the class deadline can cause a glaring need-to-be-explained hole in otherwise fine grades. And, the consequences extend to others within the young adult's sphere of influence. The occupants of the other vehicle, the friend who was planning to attend the same college, and the love interest that has some unanticipated news for both. Thus, this becomes a period of growing apart from family (physically and emotionally). The family and its resources and experience are less and less able to absorb, shield, protect and compensate for the young adult's choices and actions. At the same time, the ability to live apart from parental care and feeding becomes a necessary element of transition into becoming a mature, independent adult.

"THE BIG PICTURE" – AGE 16 to 20

VALUES: Family values are well-rooted but the opportunity for independent action requires the young adult to see consequences more clearly. Outside forces increasingly define outcomes for the child. Linkage to the favored charity is one of the very few life-long constants that enable the parents to remain "relevant," keep communication open, and stay in touch with life-directing decisions made by their child.

MISSION: Relating the philanthropic decision to course electives in school, project selections, and college major can help the parents/young adult cooperate on a long-term shared philanthropic involvement that matches up with an evolving career mission.

ACCOUNTABILITY: Important for parents to emphasize the consequences to the favored charity should the young adult "lose interest" or stop funding. Discuss expectations that have been set for the charity, and how (in necessary) to gradually redirect support away from dependent philanthropies once a new focus is determined by the young adult.

EXAMPLES OF USING PHILANTHROPY AS A TOOL

Family Values Strengthening Opportunities - Age 16 to 20

During this period, the philanthropic involvement of the heir offers several opportunities for maintaining communication and sharing interests. High school and college offer a wide range of opportunities for experimentation, and for deepening one's interest and knowledge. As mentioned earlier in the book, family values centered around open communication, and the maintenance of authentic trust, were the most important major elements in preparing heirs. The task of using philanthropy is one of continuing to define (for/with the young adult) *opportunities for expanded involvement*, or a shift to more contemporary interests that may be supportive of schoolwork or other emerging interests.

The early encouragement for the young adult to follow his/her interests (*not* the parent's interests) will now begin to pay dividends as the opportunities (and requirements) of high school and college begin to compete. Sincerely-based interests in the young adult's philanthropy will serve as a source of continuing involvement. Hopefully, during this period the philanthropy can serve as a lodestone or "hook" to provide continuity with the family and home environment.

It is now time to begin discussing with the heir the specific values that drive the family charity. While not a typical conversation, it is a conversation that successful families regularly held with their donor children. In discussing shared values, they helped the young adult begin to solidify what values are, and *why* that charitable cause attracts him/her. One excellent conversation opener is the parental statement: "...Of course, there are *several* organizations that support dolphin protection, but I am curious as

to why you support *this particular* organization?"
Families often discover reasoning that surprises
them, and reasons that reveal information about
the young adult's own developing value system.
Is the charity supported simply because it is the
only dolphin-supporting group he/she is aware
of?   Is it because it is close to home?   Is it
because a teacher or friend recommended that
particular organization?   Or because a mailing
came   to   the   child   in   connection   with   a
subscription   to   Animal   World   Magazine?
Discussing values is an abstract topic unless there
is something specific that is asked, and answered,
about a subject close to one's heart.   Then,
answers begin to pour out and the task becomes
one of sorting and prioritizing.   Simply having
the conversation is a sincere expression of interest
on the part of the parent, and expresses valuation
of the young adult's decisions to date with
respect to his/her values.

In reviewing what the researched families did,
and synthesizing it into guidance, the following
might be considered to maintain this connection
with your heir:

- Talk with your child about what
  happens to the charity when he/she
  has *less time to invest*. Ask if there is
  anything you can do to help, stating
  that you have come to value the
  charity's goals as does your child.
  Can you visit the charity and send
  information to him/her? If your child
  sits on some sort of advisory board or
  serves in a volunteer/docent capacity,
  has he/she thought about what

happens when/if they are away from home? What do others involved in the charity do when that happens?

- Discuss what a "leave of absence" from the charity's Board consists of, as opposed to a resignation simply because the involved heir is away at college, or overseas for a year of school. Encourage the child to take steps to "stay connected."

- Make certain the newsletters and progress reports of the charity are sent directly to your child, by name. And, be sure the address is changed to the college address when that change takes place.

- Ask the charity if they have any process to keep in touch with their supporters, or to be able to place their supporters in contact with one another in a nearby region. Ask also if there are specific collegiate organizations or clubs that also focus on the charity... and at what campuses.

- Specifically set aside time (not over dinner) to discuss what is happening with your child's charity of choice. Develop the information base you will need to stimulate contact (reinforcing the value of reliability and sincerity) as your child faces increasing demands on his/her time.

Mission Defining Opportunities - Age 16 to 20

This is the time when you can begin to define what the longer term missions (intentions) are for the child as well as his/her charity of choice. Is there any rationale for the child to make an effort to become more thoroughly knowledgeable and grounded in his/her field of interest? If the young adult's (unspoken) mission is to aid underprivileged children abroad, could that lead to a supportive degree in education, or psychology, or social work or international relations ? The innocent desire to help during the 5 to 10 year age period often seemed to grow into grandiose ideas during the ages of 11-15. Such ideas were reflected in a desire to "establish a clinic" or "build an orphanage" or "build a marine research foundation." By this age, (16-20) such a sense of mission has steadily moved towards more established methods of involvement such as "work abroad", "join the Peace Corps or Vista" or "serve as a lab assistant on a marine research vessel." This is not a diminished goal, or a reduced sense of mission. It is simply a view of life where the opportunity available to them is more clearly understood as one of seeking *an entry point to continued involvement*.

Several families participated in the child's financial support (matching funds, etc.) to the extent that they felt comfortable asking the charity about opportunities for their heir to participate in the charity's field activities. They simply asked if the supported organization could open a door, or set up a summer job interview, or consider the young adult's application for a temporary job in the field operation of the charity. Having supported the organization over a period of time, including volunteer office work, the value of commitment and long-term reliability often gave the family donor a substantial leg-up on the other competitors for field involvement. Such work experiences were highly rewarding in sorting out a long-term mission for the young adult. In some cases it led to decisions concerning graduate school. In every case it led to an increasingly realistic view of the young adult's long term mission in life.

This is a very important time to help these children begin to look long term, and long term for some heirs-in-waiting proved to be 3 months or less (about the length of a school quarter, or the period between vacations). Several families used the family vacation or outing together as a good example of a goal or mission. Those families asked the young adults to plan a vacation weekend. The parents remained uninvolved in the planning or reservations, etc. They allowed the young adult(s) to take over and guide the family through the vacation days together. They acceded to the youthful direction because it was part of a well thought out plan to attain their goal... the vacation at a specific spot at a specific point in time, with a specific sense of mission – to be together as a family and to reconnect as a family.

Accountability Applying Opportunities - Age 16 to 20

This is a time when successful families establish the concept of *reciprocal accountability*. It was defined by successful families as a set of "mutual obligations" that have been accepted by both parties... the donor and the donee. Families stated that they did this for **two major reasons:**

First, to avoid the feeling for their child donor of being "locked in" to a particular organization.

Often, organizations became less effective over time, leadership changes, or the criticality of the mission is reduced. When the donor became inclined to shift to a more effective support organization, he/she often felt honor-bound to continue with their original organizational selection. That viewpoint began to "sour" the donor's feeling about philanthropy in general, and their continued involvement in specific. The result: the donor drifted away, lost interest, and the family found itself holding the bag for matching funds, reliability of commitment, etc.

Second, to avoid the sense of guilt felt by their child as a donor should the young adult decide to *reduce* support. Often, difficult decisions or questions about direction and purpose for the charity arose when the charity's targets broadened, or the leadership faltered, or the donor learned of competing charitable organizations more effectively serving the same cause or mission. The families felt there was simply no logic for feeling guilty about being a financial donor, or for changing the object of the financial support.

Reciprocity of Expectations

The concept of *reciprocal accountability* proved to be an effective tool for donor families. It set the stage for the child seeing financial support as *one* form of help. Their time, another form of involvement. Their ability to attract friends and fellow participating donors, another form of support. As such, the receiving charity was regarded as *sharing the mission with the donor.* They were both headed in the same direction, and to the same destination with respect to the community served by the charity. However, shifting support in an effort to achieve (faster or more effectively) a mutually shared objective was the topic of many conversations within the subject families. This strengthened communications skills, and supported the development of *authentic trust*[31] within the family, and between the charity and the family.

> The Student Affairs Council wanted to invite a speaker to Kyra's private school, but lacked the budget to pay for transportation to and from the campus. Through the family philanthropy, Kyra (who was a member of the Student Council) made arrangements for her family to anonymously contribute some matching funds. Her ability to leverage her funds, and persuade others to contribute by supporting her interests, was a great lesson.

With respect to installing this concept of *reciprocal accountability*, it often proved effective to schedule such a conversation with the receiving charity. Such a conversation often took place at the charity's offices. The parent often *opened* the conversation by stating their gratitude for the young adult involving them in financially supporting the charity. And then, with the young adult taking the lead, inquired about future plans for the charity and how those plans

---

[31] Authentic Trust (as opposed to Cordial Hypocrisy) along with Shared Mission and Shared Values were repeatedly confirmed as a requirement for any family or team to remain united. Authentic Trust is clearly defined in *"Preparing Heirs"* ©2003 by Williams & Preisser, pages 36-41

could influence the young adult's decision to continue support, or change the support level. Thus, the concept of reciprocal accountability was opened for the young adult to take up. The steps followed by the parent and young adult can be summarized as follows:

- Express gratitude for the progress to date and express the desire to continue to be involved with their mission.

- Explain that physically, it may not be as easy to be involved, due to college distances and demands, but a desire to continue to support the mission is present.

- Request that they continue to expand their progress and effectiveness, especially when compared to other organizations with a similar mission.

- Commit to the continued support as long as their organization is the most effective organization in achieving the mission.

And thus the stage can be set for a guilt-free shifting of support if the organization does not remain self-accountable, and reciprocally accountable, to the mission and the donor. It is also a statement of self-accountability for the young adult and a declaration of reliability *as long as the charitable organization continues to perform.* It avoids a blind commitment to a future that neither can predict. It becomes a maturing event for the young adult, and sets the stage for carrying through with the charity of choice during the major changes of the college years.

Initiating Financial Responsibility Away From Home

Finally, financial structure for the young adult changes from high school to college. Funds, guidance on the usage of discretionary funds, and physical proximity to parents (in viewing the use of those funds) are altered dramatically. This is the time to sit down and *budget the philanthropic support as part of an overall expenditure/savings budget for College.* As an example, several families used the following:

- Tuition, room, board, books, and travel should be budgeted separately and a separate checking and credit card account dedicated for those expenditures. All are designated as "direct college expenses." While the young adult handles these, payments and credit card bills/bank statements are sent *to the parents'* home address.

- Personal allowance for the student should be significantly adjusted upward to include all anticipated (but discretionary) expenditures, including vehicle operating costs, off campus meals, clothing, entertainment, etc. This is a new "baseline" for allowance. Separate checking account and separate credit card with those bills sent to the *student's* college address.

- Savings, under the 1/3 rule would be separate, equal to, and *in addition* to this allowance. Deposited directly into the *student's home banking/savings account.*

- Philanthropic support would also be separate, equal to, and in addition to this allowance. Again, it is time to open a separate bank account to receive and disburse these philanthropic funds. Checks to be written by the young adult during high school and during college. Matching funds from the family philanthropy can be deposited into that account, for disbursement by the young adult donor. *Bank statements for the philanthropic account should come to the parents' home* and be reviewed with the family leader quarterly, or when the student is home on break from college.

Such an arrangement seemed to work for families who wanted to respect the young adult's increasing independence, yet remain informed on how his/her responsibilities were being handled. It also gave the family the opportunity to adjust the allowance, which, *in turn, automatically adjusted both the savings and philanthropic accounts proportionally.*

Most families anticipated a conversation during this age period concerning the question of "what can I do with my savings account? What am I saving for? When can I spend it?" "I have some real clear ideas of my own." Once again, this was a precursor to a *family conversation* about the topic. At this age, the wants center around different (and better) transportation, travel, or "items of interest[32]." The families used this as an opportunity to redefine (in conversation with the young adult) the purpose of savings, gradually

---

[32] Kayak, mountain bike, musical instrument, etc.

stepping back from any involvement with the savings-expenditure decision (usually around age 21).

Finally, this age group proved very sensitive to **hypocrisy and inconsistent application of values**. They were very open to the notion of "seeking to understand and to be understood." They *wanted and needed to be held accountable* for their choices and actions. Their family impressed upon them the consequences for their actions — both good and bad. This led to encouragement for the heir(s)-in-waiting to perform full due diligence on any funding they perform on charities. This avoided bad consequences from unintended outcomes. It proved to be an excellent tool, helping the young adult to develop the kinds of questions and demeanor that proved appropriate. This was also an opportunity for parents to remain sensitive to the roles they modeled by creating a time and place for routine continuing communication. Often the "time and place" emerged along with a family internal conflict. That conflict, if seen as a "bump in the road" that *enables* learning, invariably strengthened the family's communication skills, and their odds of post-transition success.

Chapter 8

Age 21 to 30, The Applying Years

Maximizing the Value of Contributions

Adulthood is now upon the individual, in a legal and operational sense. With the recognition of the ability to independently obtain credit cards, incur debt, enter contracts, demolish their own credit rating, and accept employment in Malaysia, the "child" is launched... whether or not we are fully prepared for that launch. Working in an organization generates a certain "shock wave" in the adult child. It literally resets all his/her evaluation metrics.

Cash (from employment) begins to flow inward to the young adult, not outward. Now, hypersensitive to what is expected of them (from others), subject to performance evaluations, and longing for the organization's approval through promotion and pay increases... the standards change rapidly. Note, the *standards* will change, not their *values*[33]. Values are fairly well set by what has gone on the first 18 years of her/his life. But now they are specifically trying to "please" and "fit in" with a new, more formal organization than their family. There is a danger of thinking "money (salary level or title) determines who I am" because of organizational culture and peer "measurement standards." Those graduates who saw money as "stored energy" seemed to fare much better, and their

---

[33] "Standards" in a company relate to job performance and goal attainment, while "values" refer to what is important to the individual such as relationships, family, quiet time, etc.

continued involvement in philanthropy helped them retain a healthy perspective.

As a parent, you cannot anticipate all the problems they will face. But, if the communication channels are open, and if questions arise from the "cold cruel workplace world," you will be seen by your child as a source of help (as opposed to a source of criticism)... in whatever form is useful to your young adult.

So, where does philanthropy come into play? It offers the *family* a method of *linking to the graduate's emerging world.* It provides a historical link to the family's values, can involve other siblings at different stages of their lives, and is associated (in the graduate's mind) with areas of mutual interest. In a way, the family philanthropy(ies) and/or a family foundation, is a timeless connection that seemed (in successful post-transition families) to be a "constant" in the relationship with parents and other family members. Ultimately, given the mutuality of interests with his/her new spouse, a family foundation offered the family member an additional way to involve the spouse into a "neutral" family element accustomed to dealing with (and welcoming) "outsiders" and "new thoughts." Clearly, an entering (new) spouse shared many of the (bloodline) heir's interests. That's one of the reasons they had become partners.

> A Word of Caution: We have observed that while the family name was a source of great pride for the parents, it could be a source of continuing (unwanted) expectations for the heirs. Seeing the family name connected with university buildings, hospitals, and community improvements often proved embarrassing to young people trying to establish "normal" relationships. It's a good idea to discuss "naming" with the entire family before parents take that step.

Now is also a time to invite the graduate into discussions about the family's need to fill longer term roles in the *family's* philanthropic leadership. The heir's solicitation of grants from the family foundation/philanthropy is often the only aspect of the young heir's experience with the family philanthropy. The policy of grant making and defining grant eligibility for a wider range of supported interests are substantially different elements. The heir needs to become familiar with broader demands, and finite family resources. Prior to this period, the young heir may have played no role in the investment policies which generate funds for the philanthropy. The heir may have never met the foundation's investment managers or understood the foundation's structure and balance sheet. The heir may have never occupied a formal role in the foundation's legal or philanthropic grant-making structure. These all offer excellent *supplementary* opportunities for involvement that can benefit the heir, and the family.

The word *supplementary* is important because it proved all too easy for families to presume upon the time and responsibilities of the graduate. The primary task of the graduate is to get personally established, settle into a life routine that is sustainable and rewarding. It is not their primary task to become re-involved in the family's priorities and daily routine. It often proved difficult for family leaders to accept that notion. The bottom line is that the family leadership should bide their time, and not try to re-involve the heir too quickly or too fully. Parents should engage in a deliberate process of *sustaining the graduate's interest* in the mission of the family philanthropy. Keep in mind that the philanthropic mission has historically encompassed charities of interest to their graduate. There is every reason to believe the graduate will welcome a more intensive re-engagement with the family (via family foundation or other family philanthropic involvement) as the anxiety of new job, new boss, new town begins to abate. Wait for that new balance point to be reached by the graduate before inviting his/her deeper (and more responsible) involvement in the family philanthropy.

"THE BIG PICTURE" – AGE 21 to 30

VALUES: Values shift toward those that are self-sustaining for the graduate. While holding on to deeper family values, a new "balance point" must be reached as an independently functioning and self-supporting individual who is beginning a family of his/her own. The heir's family of origin takes a back seat to a new partner, and gradual re-engagement in the family philanthropy will offer mutual, blended benefits.

MISSION: The awareness of clarity of mission will loom larger as the graduate realizes its importance in his/her *employer's* world as well as guidance for a new *family*. A sense of direction and continuity can be provided by continuing involvement with the family's philanthropic mission.

ACCOUNTABILITY: Reporting of donee and family philanthropic performance needs to become more formal, with higher levels of accountability made available for the graduate. The operation and measurement of the family philanthropy (as opposed to the operation of the donee organization) becomes a new and more important priority.

EXAMPLES OF USING PHILANTHROPY AS A TOOL

Family Values Strengthening Opportunities - Age 21 to 30

Successful post transition heirs were considered to be "level-headed" by their non-family peers during this period of their lives. While uniformly operating in a background of mild panic/apprehension (new job, new environment, etc.), the heirs/graduates sought to establish the beginnings of their own private/new family settings. Often this was not consciously done with respect to "family." Most often it was consciously done with respect to "spouse or partner" and to "establishing our life together." For those families/parents who had prepared their heirs for wealth and responsibility, this became a time of "helping the kids get established." The problem became one of how much help, and help of what kind?

Families who had developed and used communication skillfully, and understood the importance of well-grounded authentic trust, had relatively smooth sailing with respect to maintaining contact with their children/heirs. The graduate/heir felt no need to create distance in order to assert independence. The graduate/heir also felt no need to minimize communication with the family as a method of achieving the isolation (non-interference) for decision-making control. The graduate/heir, thus prepared, had little in the way of concerns or fears about continued parental family involvement in their lives.

Going to college, testing values, being alone, independence, fear of job seeking, followed by concerns about job performance, are all prevalent during this period. For many it also means finding a mate and for some the beginning of a family. Most do not want to take the time to be involved in philanthropic activities unless it involves their school events or a social need personally affecting them, i.e. the environment, the poor, or a current emotional, spiritual or other need. Knowing they are welcome to re-engage in the family philanthropic activities at any time is probably as important as actually doing it. (It keeps them connected to family values during this period.)

Mission Defining Opportunities - Ages 21 to 30

It is now time to focus on using the foundation to "raise the bar" concerning the sophistication of topics related to mission. For the heir/graduate, their available time became scarce, overnight. This means that parents need to assume the graduate's availability will likely be only for annual meetings of the family foundation board of directors or of the family's philanthropic leaders. With successful post-transition families, communication between the family philanthropy and its graduate/heir became more formal.

Conversations became more focused with respect to overall mission, in contrast to conversation about individual grant requests. The real goal became one of *inviting involvement of the graduate/heir (in the foundation/philanthropy/charity) over a longer term and on a more formal basis.* While some family members had no interest in such long-term involvement, most wanted to be kept informed. For heirs that declined further involvement in the family philanthropy, the use of the family foundation (as a personal developmental tool) was at an end. Those family members continued to receive summary reports of foundation or family philanthropic activities, and their re-involvement was always offered as a clear option. But, for those heirs with an *interest in remaining involved*, the family leader seemed to follow a process such as the following[34]:

Schedule a meeting time and place for you and the heir/graduate to discuss continuing involvement in the family philanthropy. Tell the graduate you would like to determine their interest in becoming a larger influence in the future of the family's philanthropies, discussing:

- Why the family engages in philanthropy.

- Why the family's leadership is important.

- How philanthropy is used to develop and prepare heirs.

Meet with the graduate/heir (an extended lunch is a non-stressful environment – do not bring documents or papers).

- Open with questions concerning the heir's continued interest in the family philanthropies, and ask how the philanthropy has helped his/her causes of special interest.

- Listen to determine if the heir's historical special interests continue or have changed.

---

[34] This is an aggregation of steps that we observed being used, and that seemed to be effective in continuing the use of the family philanthropy as an educational tool as the heir matured.

- Inquire and listen to determine interests of the heir's spouse/partner (if any).

- Listen to determine where those overall interests fit in the fabric of their everyday living – partner, job, recreation, etc.

- Open with a re-affirmation of the mission of the family wealth, its relation to the family's philanthropy. Point out that a strategy to arrive at that mission objective requires roles to be filled in the philanthropy management (or family foundation) structure.

- Describe the roles that are/will become available and seek an expression of interest from the heir.

- If no interest is expressed, comment that the option is open, and ask if he/she wishes to keep up with their special interests and reports on the status of the foundation.

- If they express interest, tell the heir that you are delighted, and will send him/her further information.

Successful post transition families did not bring any more pressure to bear than described above. Their objective was to determine if genuine interest existed, and for them to make an opportunity available... for either withdrawal or expansion of relationship to the family philanthropy.

For this age group the importance of process (to determine and define a mission) becomes the learning objective. The heir needs to appreciate the care and consensus that goes into definition of the mission for the family philanthropy. The outcome, *a consensus goal that all share,* provides a navigational tool which is referenced every time divisive forces come into play.

The unifying impact of participating in the development of a long-term mission impacted the life of the heir. Often, the heir resumed a major role as he/she entered the mentoring years (ages 30+). The practical experience of working with a clear mission, and its consensus development in this period, set the stage for such mentoring as the *heir's family required* a decade or two later. Since philanthropy itself is one of the longer-term purposes for the family wealth, the same thoughtfulness needs to go into the determination of mission for the family foundation. Major family philanthropic learning opportunities surrounding the concept of a clear sense of "mission" (for heirs who elected continued family philanthropic involvement during this age period) were reinforced by successful post-transition families using the following:

Reinforcing Leadership through Mission

Successful family leaders asked the heir to develop her/his own "checklist" for philanthropic proposals which come before the family. This provides a comparison for proposals/grant requests with the mission for the family's wealth… beginning with the heir's own favorite charities. We often observed the following in successful post-transition families:

- Asking the heir to participate with the younger children in discussing the younger children's sense of "mission" for their favorite charities. As a teacher, the older heir was asked to *help those children prepare their own proposals* to the family philanthropic grant committee.

- Asking the heir to consider *chairing the family foundation grant committee* during the 2nd and 3rd year of his/her post-graduation active involvement.

- Asking the heir to chair a *mission review committee* for the family philanthropies during their 4th or 5th year as a grant-making leadership member. The goal here is to help the heir fund his/her own family philanthropy, potentially commencing with a grant from the parent family foundation or philanthropy.

Accountability Applying Opportunities - Age 21 to 30

The notion of accountability is hitting the heir from all sides at this period of life. His/her boss, a business partner's expectations and promises, the initial efforts at being a good partner/parent/supervisor, budgets, cost management, and growth relative to peers in his/her profession. There are measurements everywhere the graduate turns, and it can be overwhelming during the first years in, and after college.

Accordingly, successful post-transition families seemed to ease off on their role in *teaching/training* of accountability (with respect to its application to the family philanthropies) and moved more into the *practice* of accountability. Accountability, as a principle, seemed to need no more reinforcement. What was needed was more *practice at application.* The family leaders often turned to the family's professional advisors, asking them to spend time working with the graduate on defining where philanthropic accountability was needed, how to clearly define what was to be measured, and how to install a tracking system in the philanthropic process:

- Professional money managers for the family were asked to teach the graduate how they selected *appropriate comparison standards* for the family philanthropy's pool of supporting investments.

- The professional investors were asked to work with the graduate to establish methods of tracking *investment performance versus standards.*

- The family's accounting firm was asked to assist the graduate in *understanding how the quarterly reports were assembled* and how they should be interpreted, and acted upon.

- The family law firm was asked to give explicit instruction to the heir concerning *key issues and laws and regulations* that can have an important legal impact on the family foundation or family contributions to philanthropy.

- The family foundation's executive director or family's philanthropic leader was asked to tutor the graduate in the practical aspects of managing the foundation on a day-to-day basis, especially what to look for with respect to:

-Minimizing administrative expenses

-Responding to changing needs and new providers

-Changing legal requirements

-Innovations reported by other family foundations[35]

The important mantra successful post-transition parents kept repeating to our researchers was "I don't overwhelm the kid… she's got lots on her plate right now." Their goal was to *retain* the interest and involvement of the graduate while maintaining *proportionality* in the background of all other events impacting the graduate's life. Loose reins, continued engagement, more listening and less telling seemed to be the keys to keeping the heirs participating in the family, even as they began to develop their own family.

This is a crucial time for these young people to not only understand they need to be accountable, but they need to hold others accountable. Philanthropic activities are a good place to ask people to be reliable, be sincere, and demonstrate *competence* by doing what they say they will do.

---

[35] Publications such as the Journal of Philanthropy and organizations like NAPP and the Family Foundation Network can be very useful to family members in managing their philanthropy. Such journals and organizations offer information that provides a sense of proportionality.

Andrew and his sister Carli both had families and children. Andrew was in medical school with 2 children, and Carli was in graduate School with 2 children. Both heirs felt overwhelmed and asked for a "time out" from family philanthropic involvement for a few years.

After Andrew started his medical practice, and Carli was established with her PhD, the two heirs gradually became more involved in the family's philanthropies. Their interests had been maintained by periodic reports from the family, even as no demands were made upon them for their time.

There will be slips and steps backward, but having the heir-in-waiting participating in the setting of standards, and consequences, proved to be an effective tool and exercise in accountability. They occasionally balked at holding others (and themselves) accountable and even had heated discussion with their parents over the issue, but ultimately expressed gratitude for the "rule of accountability" throughout the balance of their lives.

In the first meeting of the Davis family and their "coach," all family members attended. One 30-year old heir was two hours late and did not appear to have bathed for some time. He had not had a steady job since college and the family openly referred to him as "The Loser."

During 18 months of periodic family meetings to build trust and communications and to develop a family wealth mission statement, the family discovered that *because* he had no interest in the family business, *they made him feel* that "If you were not a businessman, or President, you were nobody." However, when the discussion and planning got to philanthropy, the heir saw possibilities for him to work in a different environment.

He blossomed. His energy and enthusiasm for the potential within the family foundation was contagious. He plunged into the role, working feverishly to learn more and become competent to make "good" philanthropic decisions. Eighteen months later, after a series of family meetings, the now well-groomed heir was named the President of the Family Foundation and was running 5K marathons. The transformation was truly spectacular. From *"Preparing Heirs ©2003 www.thewilliamsgroup.org*

Chapter 9

Beyond Age 30, The Mentoring Years

Unifying the Family Through Philanthropy

Here, the cycle seemed to begin anew for successful families. What was learned by the young heir during earlier years was now being taught by an adult heir and leader in his/her own family. What was important in the way of acquiring understanding and skills in administering philanthropy became secondary to the *teaching skills of the parent/adult heir.* The child's learning was addressed beginning at ages from 5 to 11, and now the new learner is the child of the now adult heir. What was learned from the parents of the heir now must be transferred to the children of the heir. This period requires a specific awareness of what has happened in the life of the adult heir, *and in the life of the partner of the adult heir.*

Often, in the relative chaos of raising one's children, it is easy to lose sight of the importance of personal introspection and reflection on how the adult heir arrived at this point in life. Special awareness of the role philanthropy played in lessons of Values, Mission and Accountability need to be clearly remembered… and understood in the light of reason. What was experienced and learned by the adult heir now must be taught to heirs-in-waiting. This is a blended responsibility for the *parents* of the heir ("…this is why I had you do it this way..") and the *heir* (…I believe *our* children will respond better to these *adjustments* based upon in the way I learned…").

The adult heir's children now need to understand the importance of their personal involvement in philanthropy... and the parents (heirs up to this time, now focusing on their own issues of transitioning wealth and responsibility) need to skillfully teach what they have learned.

The Acorn Doesn't Fall Far From The Tree

Successful post-transition family members often seemed to do a "double take" when they realized how closely they were following the patterns modeled by their parents. Often they didn't realize it until it was pointed out by their professional advisors who had spanned the generation gap. "You're following the pattern your parents set for you, don't you see..." was an often repeated phrase. Adult heirs often asked about *how to teach* their own children (heirs-in-waiting). They needed no persuasion to recognize philanthropy as a teaching tool. Having personally experienced that tool, they eagerly sought opportunities to engage their own children from the earliest opportunity. The major difference between adult heirs and their parents seemed to center in the alertness that adult heirs carried for opportunities to engage their children in philanthropy. Adult heirs seemed to listen more closely, talk more openly, and more consciously set "dinner table" expectations for their own heirs-in-waiting. In fact, the children of adult heirs were often the first to seek help from their parents as avenues for their own youthful interests... the humane society, the zoo, the children's home, the Special Olympics, etc.

"THE BIG PICTURE" – AGES BEYOND 30

VALUES: This is a time of propagating values into the adult heir's own family, using the tools for the age brackets mentioned earlier. Of special importance is the need for the adult heir and partner to have a clear understanding of their own values *as a parental couple* and this may often require some outside assistance from a mutually selected mentor.

MISSION: Over time the need to update the mission of the philanthropy will be instructive. Emerging opportunities for philanthropy will involve the heir and partner in re-evaluating priorities for their family's philanthropy, addressing new opportunities, and engaging in the refinement of a philanthropic mission with their children.

ACCOUNTABILITY: The adult heir and partner continue to set standards for accountability in organizations benefiting from their family philanthropy. What is new is the instruction of their children, and the gradual engagement of the children in philanthropy. Over time, and with the emergence of new information technologies, the opportunities for bringing the family closer to the philanthropic objectives will enhance accountability.

EXAMPLES OF USING PHILANTHROPY AS A TOOL

Family Values Strengthening Opportunities – Beyond 30

As a parent, the concept of establishing family values enters into a period of "setting the stage" and "making the values clear, by modeling those values." It's always difficult for a parent to be a teacher. However, it is inevitable that the parent will be a role model, and the children (in this case, the heirs-in-waiting) will model those parental behaviors. "We see what you *do*" is more powerful than any type of "we hear what you say." This is not a conscious effort by the children to model parental behaviors. It is picked up through the thousands of little interactions with their parents... as well as the non-interactions with a parent. Therefore, as the parent, in the "Beyond 30" bracket, this book focuses on the role that philanthropy plays in setting and strengthening family values.

Successful (heir) families were passionate about discussing their concerns over philanthropy. As part of these discussions, the children heard parents struggle with the concept of "what was the right thing to do." Deciding between grant request "A" and grant request "B" when both were aimed at accomplishing the same mission, was difficult. Successful adult heirs shared those efforts to decide, and recalled their parents efforts to make the correct decision. *From this, heirs-in-waiting learned the value that parents are not perfect, not omniscient, and that parents do not always have all the answers at their fingertips.*

Successful adult heirs talked with their children about issues of "getting the money to work in the field, on the problem." They took their time and went back to the soliciting organizations and asked for further clarification of their grant request, and for changes to their grant objectives, and for commitments to larger portions of their donation going directly to field work. *From this, the heirs-in-waiting learned the value of not being forced into a choice that is defined by others. They learned the value of defining their own choices, in their own terms.*

Successful post-transition families sought out opportunities to have their children present during the communication exchanges with charitable organizations, seekers of grants, and managers of not-for-profit institutions. *From this, and from post-discussion with their parents, heirs-in-waiting learned the values of courtesy, began to pick up on their parent's ability to "read" people, and to hear "what was NOT said" as well as beginning to evaluate the likely authenticity of "what was said". They also learned the power of the (donor's) simple request for more/different information before any grant decision could be made.*

Bill and Sallie realized during their estate planning process that the value of their estate was not only more than they needed to live comfortably, it was substantially larger than their children needed or expected. As part of their tax planning they set up a donor advised fund, and gave each child a seat on the board of the fund, announcing it Christmas Eve to all the children. They were stunned to receive thank-you notes from all of the children, and the note from one son read as follows:

"Dear Mom and Dad, I want to thank you both for the fantastic Christmas…I believe the phrase "gift of giving" is most true. Deep down I believe that there is a blessing and a benefit associated with the act of giving, and I feel fortunate that you are sharing that blessing with me …I am making my first gift of $500 to Habitat for Humanity. My commitment this year is to match your gifts by 10% to each charity I designate. This will give me an added interest and allow me, in a small way, to add a ripple of benefit to the charitable wave you have started. I am very proud to be your son and love you both very, very much." summarized from: World Vision Family Philanthropy Guidebook, p.15

In the previous example, family values were clarified, bonds into the next generation were reinforced, and the leverage of the family's wealth became apparent. Accountability and measurement ("...*match your gifts by 10%...*") emerge and philanthropy is demonstrated as a powerful teaching tool... in this case for the parents as well as their adult heirs.

Unspoken in all this is the question of "what is the 'Beyond 30' heir learning from all this?" The answer lies in the words "how to communicate." Research showed us that in making use of philanthropy as a teaching tool, the Beyond 30 adult heir learned how to mentor... how to teach... learned what tools were most effective with the heirs-in-waiting. Perhaps not surprisingly, these skills learned by the adult heir carried over into the adult heir's workplace, social settings, and community/charitable settings. Parents who worked at teaching values to their children through modeling desirable behaviors, unconsciously *carried those modeled behaviors into other organizations in which the parents participated.* Colleagues and associates of the parents were favorably influenced, as well as the heirs-in-waiting (whom they originally intended to influence).

The major lesson learned by all parties is that it was far easier to *discuss* (communicate) what tactics worked, and what tactics did not, rather than *lecture* on the subject. The parent was able to ask the heir-in-waiting what they thought of the exchange, and what they thought of how Mom/Dad handled the exchange. *From this, heirs-in-waiting learned that their opinion was important, that they had the ability to affect the future (of how their parent behaved), and that open and contemporary communication was the tool that allowed all this to happen.*

One day, in the U.S. Mail, each of 37 (related) nieces and nephews received a letter notifying them that their Grandmother's estate had made them each recipients of a $1.5 million dollar private foundation. In their 20s and 30s, they sought advice on their options which were to continue the foundation, or liquidate foundation for a charitable purpose. They decided, with some reservations, to continue their foundations and to meet quarterly.

Their first "joint board meetings" of the combined $50 million foundation(s) were polite, and generally "rubber stamped" the parents' recommendations. However, over a period of 7 to 9 years the "kids" began coming in with 15 to 20 pages of recommendations and the parents began to become a rubber stamp for the kids. The heirs learned to unify, communicate, and research for one another before making grants, and then following up on the results. As one mother said, with tears in her eyes: ..."never, in my wildest dreams, would I have believed the family would come together as they have."

Mission Defining Opportunities – Beyond 30

Once again, the adult heir had to pause, and learn *how* to define a mission for his/her own heirs-in-waiting. Although the adult heir had experienced the process personally, he/she had neither the time nor the inclination to understand what was at work at the time the philanthropy-based learning happened. Beyond 30, the process is one of *comprehending in order to teach... to communicate.* In the process of *setting policy* for the types of proposals the family wishes to consider, or the *types of programs* they wish their family to support, the beyond 30 adult heir begins to ask for *specifics* concerning the mission of the requestor. Using the family philanthropy as a leverage point, the adult heir often entered into discussions with the donee organization. The adult heir asked them to clarify their mission, and asked how that mission was defined. Finally, the adult heir would ask the following questions:

Mission-Defining Questions for Grant Requests

- Who was involved in defining your mission?

- Was the process interactive and participatory, or controlled by the largest donor or an early charter for the organization?

- What is the strategy you plan to follow to achieve that mission? Over what period of time?

- Is your operating structure such that it is designed to achieve your mission, or is it an obstacle?

- What roles are to be filled to enable that structure to operate effectively in pursuit of the declared mission?

- How will you know when the interim (and final) objectives are attained?

- What are today's plans for action you will take if you fall short, exceed, or exactly meet your mission objective?

In this dialogue, the adult heir resumes his/her learning through a more sophisticated application of philanthropy. At this stage the adult heir is becoming increasingly involved in mentoring not only her/his own children, but serves as *a mentoring force for the grant seeking organizations themselves.*

The participatory process involved in answering the above seven questions inevitably involved the adult heir in a dialogue that dealt with *the process of formulating and acting upon mission.* Mission without a strategy to attain the mission was demonstrably useless. A strategy without a structure to carry it out, and a structure without the necessary roles, competently filled, crippled execution in attaining the mission.

It became clear that a shared learning process was underway between adult heirs and the beneficiaries of the family philanthropy. This shared learning placed the adult heir in something akin to a "best practices" position. By way of illustration: When the adult heir had mission conversations with 6 to 10 different donees, the adult heir was able to pollinate their donor organization with some methodology and thinking from other non-profit organizations seeking the adult heir's financial support. In one way, mentoring of organizations (and individuals) was stimulated by the adult heir becoming a "clearing house" for information on mission, etc.

Finally, with respect to mission, the family philanthropy provided adult heirs with enduring learning where the mission *shifted* for the family philanthropy. Over time, organizations or policies became ineffective, outmoded, or replaced by new rules and regulations... which made continued support less essential. Also, in several cases, funding changed. The family's philanthropic commitments were divided among the heirs, or dissolved, or its assets diminished by giving well in excess of its investment income. In those cases, mission often had to be re-assessed and direction reset. In those families where the heirs were involved, especially in the case of mature and well-established foundations, great lessons were learned. This often provided an opportunity (for a family) to "close the door on an era." It may have been Dad's favorite charity, but Dad is no longer with the family – or the recipient organization has changed *its mission* – or new information makes support no longer appropriate. In general, the process successful adult heirs followed was as follows:

WHEN A CHANGE IN MISSION IS NECESSARY

The family leader for the charity notifies all family members (and spouses) that the topic of "Resetting the Mission" is the topic for the next family philanthropy meeting, and urges everyone to attend with their best thoughts on one of three alternatives:

1. **Hold to the same mission, unchanged**

2. **Consider a new mission**

3. **Blend points 1. and 2. making a gradual change**

- The family leader usually retains a facilitator-specialist to assist the family in defining, recording, and integrating their thoughts at the "Mission Change?" meeting, inviting the appropriate professional advisors to the family to sit in on the discussion.

- A consensus outcome was reached OR, lacking a consensus, the foundation assets were split into separate (new and old) missions.

Family members used this event to define new strategies, structure and roles for the resultant mission(s) and offered opportunities for family members to become involved.

- A written report of the "mission change" conclusions was distributed to all members, and then ratified at the following family meetings (once the legal issues were properly addressed).

Thus, even in the mentoring years, the family philanthropy provided opportunities for the adult heirs to learn, and to further mentor their own children... as well as mentor the charitable organizations supported by the family.

Accountability Applying Opportunities– Beyond 30

When a person occupies a leadership role, the question of accountability can become increasingly complicated by considerations that steadily broaden/change over time. It was not difficult to handle grant decisions when the donee failed to perform. Either the program shaped up, or the grant would be diminished, or shifted to a competing organization that seemed more likely to be successful in the mission. In fact, family philanthropies that had extensive family participation developed *stronger* internal unity as they worked through these reallocation decisions. Those decisions became a reaffirmation of the mission, reinforced family unity, cooperation, and commitment to *appropriate usage and return on the family's philanthropic funds.* Not all accountability issues are so simple.

Things become more complex, more entangled, and more likely to polarize as time goes by and people become increasingly aware of the family's philanthropic mission and its beneficiaries. No longer driven by measures of simple cost-effectiveness, a broader set of considerations often came to life; such as community involvement, competence of internal personnel and their roles in the community, public reaction to programs and policies adhered to or dropped by the family's philanthropy, etc. What was a simple decision in an earlier time ("do we or do we not support Habitat for Humanity, the home builders for the poor?") begins to take on a more complex set of considerations in a less-safe world, with a change in government, or in a partnership with a philosophically opposed organization.

Accountability standards move beyond simple quantitative measures, causing the adult heir (who may also lead a separate family foundation at this point in his/her life) to consider new elements in the accountability regime. In many cases, even though the original mission remained solidly endorsed by the family, the **public controversy** simply proved to be an element that had moved into prominence, and that the family did not wish to engage. Suddenly, the family realized that they held an *unspoken* (up to that time) *accountability standard* that was not being met, and changes were required in order to meet the (unspoken) standards. Quite frequently the issue surfaced when a regulatory or reporting requirement changed, and the privacy of the family was violated.

The philanthropically based learning for the adult heir manifested itself when the adult heir considered how to present the issue of a broken/failed (yet unspoken) accountability standard to the family. How the issues were assembled and presented; what alternatives were provided for consideration; and how much preparatory communication took place, were all important to the outcome of the family philanthropy meeting.

In 1998, Bebe Rebozo's estate bequeathed $19 million to the Presidential Library of Richard Nixon, his old friend. The 24 member Board of Directors for the Presidential Library (with names like Shultz, Kissinger, Simon, Annenberg, etc.) was overjoyed to learn of the important and needed gift, which would more than double the funds available. Since the presidential papers were still with the Justice Department, the library received no support from the National Archives, as did other presidential libraries.

However, the deceased President's two daughters were unable to agree on whether the philanthropic gift should be controlled by the Library Board or the Nixon Family. Unable or unwilling to resolve their dispute, the $19 million gift for their father's library was not accepted. Julie Nixon Eisenhower, with the support of the Library, then filed suit against her sister Tricia and the Rebozo Estate. The two daughters, who served as maids of honor at each other's weddings, remained at loggerheads over the lawsuit for 4 years.

Finally, the dispute was resolved when a Florida judge ordered face-to-face mediation, and the gift was accepted by the Library in August of 2002.

Of critical importance for the family was that *all voices were heard and considered.* No one was shut out or felt his/her recommendations were dismissed. Whatever the family decision, the (unspoken) accountability standard became spoken, and was formalized into the future standards for accountability. This provided a positive outcome from a deeper understanding and appreciation for the openness of family members. Accordingly, donee organizations were informed of the family's utilization of a new standard. This reduced their surprise factor in the event the new accountability standard was violated, advertently or inadvertently. Each participant/recipient understood the consequences of failing the new standard. In almost every case, *the new standard was verbally communicated to the donee organization's leader instead of being committed to writing.* This avoided compounding the backlash in the event support was withdrawn. After all, the families realized they were under no obligation to give. While not a legal obligation, several felt a moral obligation to gradually "phase out" support over time so alternative support could be solicited from other donors.

The lesson for the adult heir is one of *managing increasingly complex accountability standards,* and the continued involvement (education) of the family members in the decision making outcomes. Discussion in a family forum built unity, trust, and rallied the family behind the new mission that may have been required. These accountability discussions cemented values around accountability... related accountability to mission... and provided a reinforcement of family values and family unity. In fact, even a parting of ways with a long supported charity proved to be unifying for the family who made the decision as a family.

They have also learned that one must be self-accountable first and not violate their own personal value system. To miss the mark on this standard, as we all have done, they learned that there is a price to pay in dignity and self-esteem. This need for accountability has little to do with the other aspects of accountability for social or business reasons. The saying by Rob Speer

> *"...When the threshold of pain*
> *exceeds the threshold of denial —*
> *action will take place"*

is a good way of identifying the causative forces where accountability is likely to lead to action.

Chapter 10

Measuring the Readiness of Heirs

This book has focused upon how *successful* post-transition families have used philanthropy as a tool to help prepare heirs. The emphasis has been primarily on the responsibilities of the patriarch/matriarch. The establishment and maintenance of trust and communication within the family, and a program to define the mission/strategy and roles to carry out the mission are foundational. Earlier in the book (Chapter 4) a 10 Element Checklist differentiated between successful and unsuccessful (transition) families. That checklist dealt with the family as seen through *one* person's eyes (mom, dad, an heir, a spouse).

We continually heard the question: *"I know what I need to do, and what the family needs to do, but doesn't the heir have some responsibility in this preparation process?"* Summarizing what we have observed, the following list lays out the self-examination that *heirs* of *successful* wealth transition families have gone through prior to transition.

Successful families realized at some point that simply preserving wealth for the sake of wealth was not a completely satisfying goal, nor was it reflective of their personal hopes and values. They came to focus on wealth being an "enabler" of opportunities for their heirs, as opposed to being a "burden" to their heirs. As these successful families increased their emphasis on *family* while pursuing wealth-creating opportunities, they also worked at deliberately identifying opportunities for their heirs. Successful post-transition families seemed to follow this sequence:

1. Determining the "giftedness" for each heir and how, individually, they were unique in their motivation.

2. Making each heir aware that the family wanted him/her to realize their full self-potential.

3. Developing a process, within and involving the entire family, to help those heirs achieve their dreams.

4. Accepting that world events will cause "bumps in the road," change, disruption, and that the family is there to help one another learn from those "bumps."

Heirs, *when allowed*, played a critical and intimately involved role in determining their own future alignment with the family's values and mission for the family wealth.

READINESS SELF-CHECKLIST FOR HEIRS

1. Have I worked with my parent(s) and other family members to define a clear long-term MISSION for the family wealth?
2. Have I actively worked with my family to develop the STRATEGY for achieving the mission of the family wealth?
3. Have the various ROLES for the management of the family assets been identified, and do I support filling those ROLES with fully competent individuals?
4. Do I know what my PERSONAL INTERESTS are, and understand my ABILITIES well enough to identify a specific role for myself?
5. In preparing for a particular role, am I willing to be evaluated against specific observable and measurable STANDARDS?   • Education (formal and informal)   • Experience (task, competitive, charitable)   • Family Relationships (building, strengthening)
6. Have I selected a MENTOR whom I respect, who cares about my personal fulfillment, but who will be honest with me with respect to my contributions to the family mission?
7. Have I developed, with my Mentor, a specific plan to become COMPETENT for the family mission role that satisfies my interests and talents, within the mission staffing timeframe?
8. Am I EMOTIONALLY OPEN to the communications requirements and the continuing learning and evaluation that is required of each role-occupying individual within the family wealth mission structure?
9. Do I clearly understand the difference between KNOWING (what needs to be done) versus DOING (what needs to be done) and to discipline myself to act in the best interests of the mission?
10. Have I assumed personal responsibility for learning from the unavoidable "BUMPS IN THE ROAD" as demonstrated by developing (and maintaining) the skills to strengthen my family during difficult times?

©2003"Preparing Heirs"

As in earlier lists, the heir who answers "Yes" to 4 or fewer questions is very closely aligned with the *unsuccessful* post-transition families we interviewed. On the other hand, answering "Yes" to 7 or more places the heir in alignment with the *successful* post-transition families in our survey group.

Because the critical components for post-transition success involve the entire family (and spouses/partners), it was obvious that no single individual could, by their behavior alone, change the post-transition odds of success for the entire family. To change the odds took the involvement and willing participation of the entire family, usually making use of a series of skilled professional coaches.

Chapter 11

Summary and Conclusion

We surveyed 3,250 families, and 91 family foundations, and discovered that philanthropy is generally an unrecognized (yet valuable) tool for preparing heirs. This discovery had been made by the families themselves, not us. We simply documented what they had learned.

Philanthropy turns out to be one of the enduring ties between generations. It also turns out to be a powerful forum for long-term communication between the generations. As an instrument for expressing passion and interest, the emotions surrounding philanthropy are very *real*, and not contrived. Family members sense this, and learn to become open and comfortable discussing philanthropic issues.

Accordingly, family members who were mutually involved in the family's philanthropy *communicate well, listen carefully, define goals clearly, and share an expectation of accountability for the financial support they extend.* In other words, philanthropy can become the tie that binds a family together over the decades. It begins at age 5 or 6 to the mentoring that emerges from the adult heirs beyond 30 years of age. It crosses generations and holds generations together.

Never just a tax question, it became a values-mission-accountability question. Foundations established by a family solely or primarily for tax reasons tended to slowly dissemble, consolidate, or merge with other community philanthropies or foundations that were professionally managed. Family philanthropies that reflected the *passions and values of the family* endured, and became treasured vehicles for multi-generational involvement within the family. The family philanthropies also *became the point of connection between the family and other organizations that shared the family's passion...* often generating new connections and new friends sharing similar concerns on an issue.

The 10 questions that follow are representative of what successful post-transition families asked themselves *before and after* the transition event:

FAMILY PHILANTHROPY CHECKPOINTS

1	Is there a family consensus behind a written family philanthropic **mission**, consistently used to screen charitable requests?
2	Do philanthropic criteria prioritize charities that **affirmatively define** their own future?
3	Is the heir held responsible for **due diligence** on the compatibility (with the family's overall philanthropic mission) and effectiveness of each philanthropy?
4	Has the family established that **changing donee organizations** is a normal evolution process from evaluation and comparison ?
5	Does the family **meet regularly** with the heirs to review and discuss decisions, comparing the family's values to the values held by the supported philanthropy ?
6	Is each **heir** acknowledged by the family to have **leadership** and decision-making responsibility for their philanthropies ?
7	Is each heir actively encouraged to **seek input from family members** as part of a process of seeking out "best philanthropic practices?"
8	Is the concept of **leveraging family philanthropic influence** accepted by the heir, and put into practice with other philanthropic sources?
9	Is the heir responsible for identifying and sharing with the family the **learning that has taken place** as a result of the heir's experience with each charitable gift?
10	Is philanthropy **used to teach other family processes** such as personal goals, financial management skills, and the maintenance of family trust and communication?

BEHIND THE 10 CHECKPOINTS

1. This checkpoint is clearly oriented toward the concept of a family wide shared mission, and is an important concept for the heir to grasp early on. It sets the stage for "goals" and expectations for performance. Without a sense of destination, and relating that destination to the purpose of the family's wealth, the use of philanthropy as a teaching tool misses a critical opportunity. Without consensus on mission, the philanthropy itself will "drift" over time rather than being "redirected" by the family itself.

2. The notion of "affirmatively defining" their own future goes to the values held by the heir, and sets the stage for the heir rejecting the concept of "victimhood." Dealing with charities who don't make excuses, who react appropriately to changing circumstances (instead of hand-wringing and complaining), are examples of early values the heir needs to learn for his/her own self-accountability. That sense of being responsible for one's destiny (as opposed to being a "victim of circumstances") is fundamental to an heir's healthy outlook[36].

---

[36] For example, recent automobile dealer ads in California invite customers by stating a willingness to finance automobile purchases for individuals in categories such as "Bankrupt? Poor Credit? *Victim of Circumstance?*"

3. The concept of "due diligence" is nothing more than an extension of "doing your homework." Did you check out the (proposed) donee ahead of time? Do their goals match those of our family? Do they have a history of performance in our agreed upon area of concern? Are there other charities or non-profits similar to them who are more efficient and better users of resources? This teaches the donor to become self-reliant in gathering information, and not to rely solely on the judgment of others as the basis for sound decision making.

4. It is inevitable that change will occur, including change in the recipients of the family's philanthropy. Such a change may not only reflect a change in the family's goals, or commitment of support, but also can reflect a change to a more effective donee organization. This can occur because another organization has become more efficient, the problem may have been solved, or a more needy donee or cause has been embraced. In any event, the heir needs to learn to carry a sense of obligation to the goals, and not necessarily an obligation to the donee organization.

5. Regular meetings keep the heir(s) in touch with the family mission and the agreed-upon philanthropic objective. And the meetings keep the heir in contact with the family in a group or family setting. Communication skills were practiced, new passions and interests were brought to the surface, and family unity was strengthened. Regular meetings also allowed preparation time and caused more thoughtful dialogue to take place among the family members.

6. While others may share the load (and the interest in the charitable objective) with the heir, the ultimate responsibility for the heir's decision, and its outcome, remains with the heir. Families honored the heir's decision to support a particular philanthropic objective even if they disagreed with some of the donee's goals or competencies. The learning goal here is to have the heir shoulder responsibility for a particular area of interest that the heir advocated. That responsibility cannot be diverted, assumed by another, or ignored. If the responsibility is not shouldered by the heir, then the heir must accept that the family has no "reciprocal responsibility" to help with the heir's philanthropy of choice.

7. Quite often family members have learned novel processes or techniques from philanthropies that they individually support. Accordingly, in the family review meeting format, there is an opportunity for learning and sharing "best practices" that are known within the family unit. The sharing of knowledge, respectful listening, and the give and take of questions and answers all proved to be major contributors to communication skills. Philanthropies are so often "matters of the heart" that conversations can move beyond even the "spirited" level. This provides learning with respect to patience, paraphrasing the arguments of another, and seeking compromise as a way of reaching shared conclusions.

8. Leverage is a way to multiply the expertise and funds that an heir brings to bear upon a philanthropy of interest. Learning what works, and persuading a like-minded friend to join in your support, proved to be a relatively exhilarating experience for heirs. It taught them certain business and management lessons in the power of affiliation, team effort, and magnified "purchasing power." Most of all, the heir learned that their influence was proportional to the knowledge, money and attention they brought to the philanthropy, and not all of it had to be

her/his own. An excellent example of this is related in Appendix E which tells of the leveraging power of one young woman's accomplishments relative to saving wild cats, and doing it so efficiently that other donors shifted their funding to her organization.

The Rios family authorized each of their college age children to designate $20,000 per year to the philanthropy of their choice. One child, Ashley, chose to contribute specifically to an Arts and Music program at the (only) K-8 school she had attended in her local community.

The cultural programs blossomed and had an unexpectedly large (and beneficial) impact on the learning and cultural atmosphere of the entire school.

With no guarantee that the gift would be continued, the students and their parents decided to do their own fund-raising. The very next year they raised $100,000 on their own, as evidence of the importance of Ashley's initial gift.

---

9. Reviewing what has been learned, in a family meeting setting, proved to be very maturing for the heir(s). In fact, it proved doubly effective when the parents were able to share some of their own learning and everyone became comfortable at being a "beginner" at something. For the heirs to discover that learning was a

function of newness and involvement, and risk (rather than continuing to believe that learning diminishes with age) proved to be an eye-opener. It made it easier for the family to communicate, express misgivings and kudos, and accept that while mistakes are an inevitable part of life, learning is optional and available to anyone who seeks it.

10. Finally, what is learned from the involvement in philanthropy seemed to extend easily into other useful lessons in the heir's maturation process. Financial management and tracking skills, the notion of accountability, a willingness to change horses as required, building a team that is unified behind a set of goals, evaluating effectiveness, listening and communicating, awareness of shared mission, all seemed to percolate well into other family and business arenas. In a number of cases, participation in a philanthropy often resulted in a Board Seat governing the philanthropy. That seat, in turn, provided tangible benefits in networking, shared passions, and wider links in relationships for the heir(s).

Final Thoughts

The preparation of heirs for the post-transition world of wealth and responsibility is critically important. It is important for the family who seeks the best for their children, and as a country that hopes for the best in the use of its resources. Preparation is the difference between the 70% of post-transition families whose assets and/or unity begin to disintegrate shortly after estate transfer, and the 30% who remain unified as they prosper.

Thoughtful, family wide participation in philanthropy leads to growth in self-esteem, stability, imagination, and a rewarding family life. And, as research indicates, the adult philanthropist becomes the values model for the children/heirs of the upcoming generation. While well-managed assets generate the earnings that can support philanthropy, and tax incentives stimulate its consideration, *the learning that is possible for the heirs can be the single most powerful outcome.*

Prepared heirs more readily and appropriately manage their own future, are better equipped concerning their future competitiveness, and are more thoughtful leaders concerning the opportunities for the *next* generation of heirs. Philanthropic involvement, beginning at an early age, is a wonderful and historically overlooked tool in attaining those goals.

We welcome any comments, examples, and contributions you may offer for the next edition of this book.

Roy Williams   *Vic Preisser*

for

The Leadership Family Institute ©2003

(a tax-exempt Foundation for

Post-Transition Research and Education)

APPENDIX A

Roy Williams and Professor Newman Peery of the Eberhardt School of Business at the University of the Pacific (Stockton, CA) sampled wealthy individuals who were believed to be concerned about philanthropy and family values. These families received a 110 question survey divided into 6 sections:

1. Background information about experience in philanthropy

2. The use of family foundations

3. Attitudes about wealth

4. Young adults' experience with volunteer activity and philanthropy

5. Perceptions concerning skills that can be developed through philanthropic activities

6. Values

The questionnaire was sent to 413 individuals selected from a list of persons who attended a conference sponsored by The Gathering in September of 1995 and from a list of clients of The Williams Group. Completed questionnaires were received from 89 individuals which resulted in a 22 percent response rate, considered good for this type of survey research.

The data in the study was first subjected to a statistical technique called Factor Analysis. This approach is used to identify questions or scale items which can be used reliably to identify and measure the underlying concepts of the study. The Factor Analysis resulted in the identification of seven factors listed below, which included the degree to which, the respondent:

1. values privacy

2. has confidence that if personal wealth were lost it could be regained

3. was encouraged early to engage in philanthropy or volunteer activities

4. and members of the family were involved with family foundation activities

5. had experience in philanthropy measured in years, number of projects, expenditure of personal time and energy in projects

6. and family had personal direct involvement in reviewing grant proposals and decision-making concerning which philanthropic projects to support, and

7. used wealth for philanthropic purposes to achieve personal goals and values concerning a better society

The variables defined in the factor analysis were then subject to multiple correlation analysis as shown in the following table. These correlations were checked to see if they were statistically significant, that is, the degree to which the results could have been expected to occur merely by chance. While the level of significance of the study was set at 5%, higher levels of significance were found in many of the relationships. The level of significance, or *p value*, is shown as the following in the table:

- $p < 5\%$ = +
- $p < 1\%$ = ++
- $p < 1/10^{th} \%$ = +++

Multiple Correlations Among
Variables Related to Philanthropy

	1.	2.	3.	4.	5.	6.	7.
1. Value Privacy							
2. Confident of regain wealth							
3. Encouraged as young adult in philanthropy		+					
4. Involved in Fam Fdn		+					
5. Experience in Philanthropy			++	+			
6. Personal involve in Philanthropy			++	+++	++		
7. Used wealth for Philanthropic purposes	+	++	+++	++	++	++	

APPENDIX B

Sources behind the 70% Failure Rate for Post-Transition Families and their Assets

The 70% Failure Rate (For Family Businesses) Transitioning to the Next Generation

> Below is a sampling of quotations regarding the 70% failure rate in transitioning wealth. The combination of (1) the reluctance of successful families to submit to interviews, and (2) the disinterest of researchers to investigate wealth transfer in this small population made cross-linked data hard to obtain. The Williams Group interviews of 3,250 successful families confirm a post-transition failure rate between 65 – 75%.

"Although well over 90 percent of all corporations (and many of the largest public corporations) in the U.S. are family owned or controlled, the average life expectancy of such organizations is only twenty-four years, and only three out of ten family firms survive into the second generation. Of the 70 percent that do not survive into the second generation, many could survive if only the owner/managers better understood the key issues involved in managing change and if they were better equipped with some change strategies to handle the process of adaptation and continuity more effectively."

SMR Forum: "Managing Change in the Family Firm – Issues and Strategies",
Beckhard, R. and Dyer, W.G., Jr.,, Sloan Management Review, 24:3 (1983 Spring)

"Despite the prominence of family firms, leaders of family businesses have had difficulty managing them successfully over time; many go out of existence after ten years, and only three out of ten survive into the second generation. . . .One thing we've concluded is that family-owned businesses would benefit considerably from explicit planning worked out by the founder with the family."

"Managing Continuity in the Family-Owned Business",
Beckhard, R. and Dyer, W.G., Jr.,
<u>Organizational Dynamics</u>, Summer 1983, Vol. 12, No 1., 1983,
5-12

"A family business owner who intends to pass his or her business on to future generations faces a unique set of challenges. According to the 2002 American Family Business Survey conducted by the Mass Mutual Financial Group and the Raymond Family Business Institute, only 30% of family businesses will survive the initial transition from the founders to the second generation. Moreover, only 30% of those businesses that survive the initial transition will survive the subsequent transition to the third generation."

"The Family Constitution: An Important Wealth
Preservation Tool",
London, Johanna J., Michael Best & Friedrick LLP, Attorneys
at Law publication Feb 2004

"In family firms, the problem of succession and continuity acquires an even greater significance. Consider the following findings: Available estimates (Dun & Bradstreet, 1973) indicate that approximately 70 percent of all family firms are either sold or liquidated after the death or retirement of their founders (Beckhard and Dyer, 1983). The failure of these businesses to continue as family firms beyond the tenure of their founders has serious social and economic consequences."

"The Succession Conspiracy", Lansberg, Ivan,
<u>Family Business Review</u> Summer 1988, Pages 119-143

"With fewer than 1 in 3 family firms surviving to the second generation, and fewer than 1 in ten making it to the third, the stakes are huge."
Paul Karofsky, Executive Director of the
Northeastern University Center for Family Business,
Time.com,
"Growth Drives Family Firms Crazy," March 17, 2001

"According to Niemann (Michael Niemann, director of the St. Louis office of Arthur Andersen Center for Family Business), two out of three of these businesses don't make it from generation one to generation two."
"Dad to Step Down at 35 percent of Family Businesses"
by Ron Janecke - St. Louis Business Journal - March 31, 1997

"To this day it remains exceptional for families to retain great wealth for more than three generations, if not always for the reason Smith suggested."
The Economist, June 16, 2001 –
"The New Wealth of Nations"
by Matthew Bishop, page 4

"The Chinese have a saying, 'Fu bu guo san dai,' or 'Wealth never survives three generations.' America has its own version of this saying: 'From shirtsleeves to shirtsleeves in three generations.' As with most old proverbs, there is a grain of truth to this – and the new rich are searching for ways to avoid history's curse."
The Economist, June 16, 2001 –
"To Have and To Hold"
by Matthew Bishop, page 7

"Carefully conducted studies are few and far between because data on family involvement is scarce, but those studies that do exist seem to suggest that well over half of family business assets do not stay under family control through a second generation.
"Preparing Heirs – Successful Estate Plans
for Wealthy Families Require Open Communication,
Participation Across Generations",
Stanford Business, May 2004, Volume 72,
Number 3, Page 18-20

"...only one third of businesses successfully make the transition from each generation to the next... and that figure has been very stable, and is true around the globe..."

Prof. Joe Astrachan, Cox Family Enterprise Center
Kennesaw State University, GA
The Economist, p 69, 6 Nov 2004

APPENDIX C

Selecting a Family Coach

What are the Critical Attributes of a Competent Family Coach?

Often a family coach is a skilled practitioner who has evolved from another professional field. He or she may have previously been a clinical psychologist, or an estate planner, or even a medical doctor. But all successful coaches will have evolved the following identifiable characteristics:

- They are <u>not judgmental</u> or critical. They simply want the best outcome for your family.

- They have developed <u>a consistent process,</u> and are capable of explaining that process in a manner you can understand.

- They <u>build skills</u> with your family members in areas necessary for a successful transition of your family wealth. They do not stop their work once the answer is found, but instead *continue their work until the family is proficient in the skills* required to install (or implement) the answer.

- They have a <u>"track record" of successful families</u> who are willing to serve as a reference for them.

- <u>You feel comfortable and confident</u> when talking with them.

- <u>The Coach is part of a larger team</u> and has a spectrum of resources from which he/she can draw.

Very rarely does one specific coach possess all the skills needed to lead a family through the process of preparing for a transition...preparing the heirs. The process often requires a team – an assembly of experts in philanthropy, investments, trust and communication, preparing heirs, and mission development. These components all require different skills. Skills so critical to the long-term growth and success of a family that the Lead Coach cannot be a beginner or minimally competent. Effective coaching is based upon field experience in coaching families (in a family dynamics setting, not an individual counseling setting) as well as research that provides continuation of the coach's learning. The family needs coaching virtuosos and masters, people who are continually designing new processes and techniques, and who are investing in further knowledge in the field; coaches who want to become increasingly skilled in assisting with the breakdowns that occur within families.

How can My Family Select a Family Coach?

When we reviewed the research results, comparing families who successfully transitioned their wealth versus those who did not, certain aptitudes of the family coaches who were used began to surface. The qualifications listed in the section above were routinely present among the competent family coaches. *The successful families had family coaches who emphasized the following aspects of their family coaching process:*

- <u>All</u> family members were interviewed or involved in the coaching sessions (including spouses and children over age 15) to determine their individual needs.[37]

- A family wealth mission statement was developed early on, using input from <u>all</u> the family members and arriving at an early consensus.

- Issues of trust and communications were addressed and <u>practiced</u> within the family, under the supervision of the coach.

- Issues of the competence[38] required of heirs were discussed and a plan for attaining heir competencies was <u>implemented</u> and followed.

- The establishment of a mood that welcomed declarations of "I am a <u>beginner</u>" encouraged family members to learn and grow.

- One outcome of effective coaching was that it was seen as a distinct "plus" by estate planning professionals and financial advisors, and in fact <u>reduced the costs</u> of other long-term professional assistance (legal, accounting, etc.).

- Another outcome was that the family felt better qualified in the process of <u>selecting and evaluating professionals</u> to assist the family in other matters.

The above experiences correlated well with successful family coaches and might be seen as

---

[37] It was effective only if the polling was done in person.
[38] Family members need to self-classify with respect to "competence" at a particular task. It was often effective to use verbal equivalents such as "Beginner" or "Novice" with series of progressive (verbal) levels leading to "Expert" or "Master." This enabled members to quantify their personal competence levels without embarrassment. *"For Love & Money,"* Monterey Pacific Publishing, 1997, pages 102-103

"reference questions" that would provide a family with a baseline concerning evaluating a prospective coach. A critical aspect of the above listing confirms that the easier decision to NOT involve the entire family (for scheduling or other reasons) often proved consistently detrimental to successful family transition planning. Other coach elements, such as age, gender, length of time in the field, all seemed to relate more closely to the overall family comfort level, especially with the patriarch-matriarch leaders. The three latter factors did NOT correlate with either success or failure of the family coach.

APPENDIX D:

Comments on **Mentoring** Heirs
From *"PREPARING HEIRS"*©2003 p. 144

Question 6. Have I selected a Mentor whom I respect, who cares about my personal fulfillment, but who will be honest with me with respect to my contributions to the family mission?

Here we imply the requirements of shared respect between the heir and the mentor, a concern for the personal well being of the heir, and complete honesty (and often, complete confidentiality) with respect to whether or not the heir is "making the grade" with respect to preparing for and supporting the family mission. Important to this process is personal evaluation of the heir's level of competence, which the coach/mentor will be continually assessing.

The mentor should not be a peer of the heir, and should not be selected on the basis of friendship. The mentor should be older than the heir, certainly more experienced, and skilled at drawing the heir into the self analysis and objectivity needed to understand the heir's progress toward competence. The self-esteem of the heir needs to be the mentor's first concern, with the understanding that self-esteem can only arise from thoughtful preparation, overcoming obstacles, and being recognized as a contributor to the family mission. Competence developed by the heir will lead to confidence. Confidence inevitably leads to self- esteem. It is a positive reinforcement sequence.

A reminder here might be in order: The heir must have been actively involved in the development of the mission for the family and its wealth. There should be no question concerning the heir's support for the family mission. If there is a question about the heir's support, that is the first aspect that needs to be addressed with the mentor, since it might be evidence of insincerity, show a lack of comprehension, or be a result of non-participation. Mentors are tutors. Mentors are active counselors who are paid from the family wealth, *but who are responsible to the heir, not the family.*

The mentoring process in successful families was initiated by an extensive initial interview with the heir[39]. This provided the mentor with a deeper understanding of the environment and the relationships. Thenceforth, the contact between the mentor and the heir was both scheduled (progress evaluations), and episodic, in response to a need of the heir ("I have a question," or "a change has occurred").

Mentoring continued for 1 to 3 years… or as long as 10 or 20 years. As time passed, the relationship and the bond between the mentor and heir deepened, but it was important that the mentor remained professionally uninvolved with the family assets.

---

[39] A series of lesser interviews with other family members and spouses had already been performed as part of the family wealth mission statement preparation.

No confusion was allowed concerning the mentor's primary obligation (to the heir), and that priority of the heir was not compromised by any involvement of the mentor with the family's financial or business assets. The family had already entrusted their most valuable asset to the mentor....their heir.

APPENDIX E

SAVING THE WORLD'S WILD CATS – A Young Woman's Passion

Kristin Nowell loved her pet cats as a child, and that seed grew into a passion and a mission. While **attending Stanford University** she took time out from her studies to work actively with cats. Darting feral cats (Felis domesticus) in her apartment's backyard with a veterinary blowpipe, she then took them to the clinic where she worked. Her real interest, however, lay in contributing to the survival of endangered wild cats – big cats, like tigers and jaguars, as well as small, like ocelots and marbled cats. Soon after graduation she moved to Namibia, Africa, and spent four years studying cheetahs. Those were some of the best days of her life, observing and following cheetahs as they roamed across the African plains in their daily struggles of survival, but she knew that these beautiful cats could well disappear if something wasn't done to kickstart global interest in conserving these exquisite predators in the wild.

She was invited to join the international philanthropic network of leading cat experts, the Cat Specialist Group of the World Conservation Union's Species Survival Commission. She served as its Vice Chair for Projects and also on its steering committee. Working closely with Chairman Peter Jackson, she spent five years compiling all available information about the status and conservation of the world's 36 species of wild cat. This 406 page book[40], known as the "Cat Action Plan," became the worldwide handbook for cat specialists and is regarded as the authoritative reference for the family Felidae.

Kristin's work taught her some important lessons about **values** (what is important in her life), **mission** (to find a way to preserve cat species), and **accountability** (what organization was doing the best job for the money it was spending).

Not satisfied with the answers to the last two questions, she plunged into undercover work to define the poaching and distribution chains for illicit animal trade, was featured in **Time Magazine**, established a wildlife trade monitoring office in Taiwan (TRAFFIC Taipei), and applied her knowledge to the international politics of sanctions. She helped pioneer what has become standard practice in conservation today: *working with poachers to convert them to wildlife protectors by replacing the meager income they used to derive from hunting (endangered species) with income from protecting, guiding, and researching.*

Leveraging her philanthropic involvement, Kristin wanted to support the work of cat specialists around the world, especially in developing countries. In 1996 she established the Cat Action Treasury (CAT), a nonprofit fund for wild cats in their natural habitats. CAT focused on funding the conservation goals in "the big book" (the Cat Action Plan). Since

---

[40] "Wild Cats: Status Survey and Conservation Action Plan", 1996, K. Nowell & P. Jackson, 406 pp, IUCN-The World Conservation Union, Cambridge, U.K., $40 (U.S.). The full book is also available free, in its entirety, electronically at <www.felidae.org>

then, CAT and Kristin have made remarkable advances in helping improve the situation of the world's wild cats. CAT has organized projects for tigers in Cambodia and Burma; snow leopards in Nepal; cheetahs in Pakistan; clouded leopards in Thailand; lions across Africa; and made huge advances in scientific knowledge about the little known small wild cats – the Andean mountain cat, kodkod, black-footed cat, Borneo bay cat, Chinese mountain cat, Asiatic golden cat, and more.

With her focus on mission, and her insistence on accountability, donors - including individuals, private foundations, governments, and corporations - began to see that their highest "return on (philanthropical) investment" was with this small and efficient CAT foundation. Exxon/Mobil (which has the tiger as its corporate logo) and others saw that their money went directly to wild cat conservation projects, and not primarily to administration. Governments and park managers around the world have refocused their efforts to conserve the world's wild cats, based on CAT's leadership. Kristin Nowell's philanthropic lessons learned (with respect to values, mission, and accountability) attracted and led to a dramatic surge of interest and passion for saving rare and beautiful wild cats.

You are invited to visit CAT's website at **http://www.felidae.org** if you are interested in supporting Kristin. or working hands-on in international wild cat conservation.

APPENDIX F

Resources from *The Williams Group*

BOOK: "FOR LOVE & MONEY"

A Comprehensive Guide to the Successful Generational Transfer of Wealth By: Roy O. Williams -This book contains the detailed philosophical underpinnings behind the "Wealth Transfer Pyramid" and is especially useful to the reader seeking more foundational thinking.

> Cost: $29.95 per copy + $4.50 shipping and handling for first copy; $3.00 shipping for each additional copy to same address. Volume discounts available

BOOK: "PREPARING HEIRS"

Five Steps to Successfully Transition Family Values with Family Wealth By: Roy O. Williams & Vic Preisser -This ground-breaking book distilled the differences in 3,250 families that transitioned their wealth. In looking at the differences between the 1,000 successful families and the 2,250 unsuccessful families the authors developed *a series of 10 Question checklists that let a family member quickly assess the odds of a successful transition.* Not an estate planning book, but a post-transition planning book that should be in the hands of every estate planner.

> Cost: $29.95 per copy (same shipping and handling costs as above)

50 QUESTION TRANSITION READINESS SURVEY:

A 50-question anonymous Survey, completed by *all family members and spouses,* submitted to The Williams Group for analysis and scoring. The result is a detailed written report of the differences within the family that threaten a successful post-transition. Anonymity of respondents is protected. All participating family members receive a copy of the 8 page customized report.

> Cost: $500 per entire family of 7
> (+$50/person beyond 7)

CONTACT: *thewilliamsgroup.org*   or   209 477 0600
3620 West Hammer Lane, Stockton, CA 95219